Markets, Consumers and Firms

Theme 1 for Edexcel AS and A Level Economics B

Brian Ellis

Nancy Wall

Brian Ellis has been involved in teaching, examining, curriculum development, teacher training and writing. He sees it as important for people to think and to smile sometimes.

Nancy Wall taught for 15 years and then worked in curriculum development, with a particular interest in teaching strategies and teaching resources. She is reviews editor of 'Teaching Business and Economics', the magazine of the Economics and Business Education Association (EBEA) and Treasurer of the Association for European Economics Education. She has long experience of writing and editing resources for students.

Acknowledgements
The authors were able to build on some of the work done earlier by Polly Glegg for Anforme publications. This has been helpful. They are also grateful to the many small businesses that have figured in the case studies. (Not all of these are appearing under their actual names.)

Every effort has been made to trace the owners of copyright material that is reproduced here, but in a very few cases this has not been possible. We offer our apologies to any copyright holder whose rights may have been unwittingly infringed.

Anforme Ltd, Stocksfield Hall, Stocksfield, Northumberland NE43 7TN.

Typeset by George Wishart & Associates, Whitley Bay.
Printed by Stephens & George Print Group, Merthyr Tydfil.

Contents

Using this book

'Markets, Consumers and Firms' sets out basic economic ideas alongside the real world of business. The insights of economic theory are used to analyse consumer and business decisions. The broader context of the economy, society and the role of government is also examined so that students who are beginning this course develop an appreciation of the economic relationships that underlie all the decisions that have to be taken.

Every chapter starts with a case study. Wherever possible these are real-world stories, or based on a business that is well known to the authors. Occasionally the real world has to be simplified in order to ensure that readers are not overwhelmed by the inevitable complexities.

Watch Out! Notices in some chapters will alert readers to common problems that require a little extra thought in the study process.

Questions

Most chapters end with questions that follow the format used in exam papers. The majority of these are data response questions; a few are extended writing questions of the type to be found in exam section C of Edexcel's AS and A level Economics B course. We see these questions very much as part of the learning process. In due course the publishers will make answers available for most of the questions. But always be aware that there is much more to say besides what appears in official answers, and often, several ways to get a good mark.

We have tried to focus on the ideas that students will already have learnt, so that these questions do not require prior knowledge that they do not yet have. However real exam questions will often require answers using a wider range of subject content, so these particular questions will seem rather narrow in comparison. Students who are revising for imminent exams must be ready for questions that require breadth of understanding across the whole course and should consult the Edexcel website for specimen assessment materials or past papers.

Looking into the future!

In thinking about what you are learning, be alert to the world around you. We live in very interesting times, with much change in the global economy and the world of business. Keeping a close watch on the economic and business environment will help you to understand the relevance of what you are studying. Events are like a serial and sometime we want to see around the next corner, understand the way things are going and link up causes and consequences. This can be exciting as well as, sometimes, quite an anxious experience. There is a real chance that you will emerge from this course with a great feeling of being able to understand some of what is happening. The authors really want you to enjoy this process and wish you the very best of luck with your studies.

Chapter 1

The economic problem

Stonehenge

There are many theories about Stonehenge. Our ancient monument may have been a primitive computer for calculating seasons and eclipses, a healing centre, a place of worship or a burial site – or some combination of these. The stones were erected 4,000 to 5,000 years ago. The earliest signs of activity in the area go back around 10,000 years. There are no written records from the Bronze Age, so we cannot be sure of what was going on or why this site was important. We do know that the larger stones are around 8 metres long, 2.5 metres wide and 1.5 metres thick. The biggest of them weigh 50 tonnes. Transporting the stones was no easy business; some came from Wales, for example. There were few basic tools and only human power. There were three phases of construction, estimated to have required more than 30 million hours of labour in all.

Choices

Successive generations made the choice to devote extensive resources to construction. We don't know if everyone was enthusiastic about this or if the workers were simply earning a wage (or were slaves). Our image of Bronze Age people as primitive and struggling to survive is challenged by Stonehenge. They had sufficient resources, organisation and skills to tackle this project. They must have chosen to give up many other useful activities in order to achieve what they did. Making choices about alternative uses of scarce resources is at the heart of economics. After many generations of progress, we still make choices and every choice still means that alternatives are given up.

> ### Discussion points
> 1. How can we be confident that Stonehenge was important to the people who built it?
> 2. Some ancient human remains at Stonehenge came from people born in Germany and near the Mediterranean. Are you surprised by that?
> 3. How different were the needs of Bronze Age people from your needs now?
> 4. How important do you think Stonehenge is now?

Scarce resources

Few things are available in unlimited quantities and even fewer are unlimited and useful. Bronze Age people probably regarded fresh air and perhaps water as freely available in unlimited quantities. Neither of these examples looks very safe today; we see these things as more finite (not unlimited). Millennia ago, as now, human labour must have been a scarce resource. Using people's time in one way has the consequence of requiring us to give up anything else which might have been done instead. In some ways, Bronze Age people gave up less. They didn't have the options of Facebook or of the cinema, for example. However, we assume that they were far poorer than we are, so devoting time to building Stonehenge could have used up energy needed to obtain food or shelter or even to survive. We believe that meeting basic needs took up most of their time. The best alternative we give up when we make a choice is called the **opportunity cost**. By choosing to study economics, we give up alternative subjects and perhaps also alternatives to study.

Opportunity cost

> **Think!**
>
> What is the immediate opportunity cost of your reading this today?
>
> What is the opportunity cost of having chosen Economics?
>
> Who can you think of who has given up a really attractive alternative by making a choice?

> Anything useful which is not available in unlimited quantities is a **scarce resource**.
>
> Using a scarce resource in one way means we sacrifice alternative uses. The best alternative given up is called the **opportunity cost**.

⚠ WATCH OUT!

Scarcity in economics does not mean very rare, like diamonds or a four leaf clover. It means there is limited availability and so an opportunity cost when one use is chosen, in preference to another.

Choice

The problem of scarcity is central to economics. Human needs are unlimited – most of us can think of more things that we want. But resources are finite (not unlimited) and when we use them in one way they are normally not available for other purposes. So **choices** must be made. As consumers we base our choices on personal preferences, within the constraint of our incomes.

Scarcity

You can see at once that scarcity is more of a problem for individuals if they have relatively low incomes. In all societies some people have higher incomes than others. There are individuals who might have all the material things they desire; they are not necessarily the richest people. Even those people have limited time and cannot do everything.

As consumers we base our choices on personal preferences, within the constraint of our incomes.

In economics we try to work systematically, and even scientifically. The physical sciences, such as chemistry and physics, work from observation and experiments to build up understanding. Human behaviour is very complex and also changes with the time and place. This means that economics often works with less certainty than physical scientists have about, say, gravity or the chemical composition of a substance. We often work from simplifying assumptions and build up theoretical models.

Our starting point in economics is entirely realistic. Because resources are finite, we have to make choices and to accept that the choices we make have opportunity costs. As a society, we cannot have everything that we need and want. Scarcity is a problem for society as a whole, as well as for the individual.

Income

> Resources are nearly always scarce, in relation to the use that we can make of them and so choices must be made. Choices will be constrained by our level of income and the opportunities we face. As consumers we decide what to buy. We also decide how to allocate our time. Businesses and governments also face choices.

Besides choosing what to consume, individuals also choose how to organise their lives around work, leisure and other commitments. Opportunity cost is about time as well as resources. Furthermore, it applies to any human organisation. In fact the most fundamental choices that we see being made within the economy fall into three categories:

● *What do we choose to make?* Will driverless cars become the norm? Or is it more important to have a good bus service? Might it be possible to have both?

● *How do we choose to make it?* This is a decision for the producers, the businesses that decide on the best way of creating the product. It may have a big effect on society: more automated processes in industry might mean fewer jobs but lower prices.

● *Who is it for?* Who will benefit from these decisions? Being able to choose to buy what you want is a valued personal freedom for us all, but what if we are homeless and penniless? We might settle down to selling the Big Issue, but it may be better for society if the government sets up systems to protect people from the worst that can happen.

Show your understanding

Are you planning to go to university? What will the opportunity cost be? Now take the other view. For you, what might be the opportunity cost of *not* going to university?

Choices in business

Trade-offs

People in business are faced with constant choices. We can start with the simplifying assumption that enterprise is motivated by profit. We can then modify our assumptions to add more realism. What should the business produce? One answer would be the product that is likely to be the most profitable. A product that is really popular with the customers is likely to be profitable. But customers may be quite fickle; they may be on the lookout for something new and interesting. The opportunity cost of concentrating on the most profitable line might be being unprepared for a change in consumer preferences.

Businesses often use a different way of looking at opportunity cost: sometimes it is better to think in terms of **trade-offs**. A taxi driver might consider a trade-off between how many hours he works and how much income he makes. He has to balance the need to earn against his preference for taking things easy. In a different context, there may be a trade-off between speed and accuracy in any kind of work.

> Like opportunity cost, a **trade-off** involves choice. We often use the term trade-off when looking at a balance between two choices, choosing more of one and less of the other, rather than making a simple either/or choice.

The economic problem

Facts

Evidence

Values

Think!
Young professionals face a trade-off between commitment to their jobs and their social life. They frequently accept working for very long hours early in their careers, but find the trade-off against other activities harder as years go by. Can you understand this? Is it likely to apply to you?

The economic problem requires that choices be made to decide how to use finite resources to best effect when our wants are effectively unlimited. Consumers, producers and governments all face choices and trade-offs. Choices often entail judgements which depend on opinion rather than established facts. Two people watching television together might prefer to watch different programmes. Two politicians might disagree on the relative importance of nuclear weapons and of care for the elderly. When we are dealing with facts that can be tested, we call this **positive economics**. Where judgements and opinions are involved, we call this **normative economics**. The boundary between positive and normative is often clear, but there is a risk of confusion.

Positive statements in economics are testable as factual or false, normally on the basis of observation and evidence.

Statements about the economy which depend on opinion and judgement are referred to as **normative**. They often involve ideas on what should be done. They are sometimes called value judgments.

Try this
1. Think about the difference between what you need and what you want. Do you have needs different from those of Bronze Age people?
2. Would you agree that needs are positive whereas wants are normative?

Choices that face governments

We encounter a great many political issues that are strongly normative! In fact party policies are usually based on beliefs about what should happen, despite all the evidence that politicians so often refer to. But even where the choice of policy is bound to be a matter of opinion, we can still find trade-offs that have a strong factual element.

Show your understanding
For each of these statements, say, is it positive or normative. If there is a trade-off involved, explain how and why.

● We could scrap Trident and use the money saved to build more affordable housing.

● House prices have risen because it is difficult to get planning permission.

● Educational standards would rise if school classes were smaller.

● Waste recycling is expensive and ineffective.

Exam style question

Health spending

Country	Average life expectancy (years)	Share of income spent on health (%)
Brazil	74	9.3
India	66	4.0
Japan	84	10.1
South Africa	56	8.8
United Kingdom	82	9.4
United States	79	17.9

Source: World Bank

The data in the table above shows relatively long life expectancy in the United Kingdom, suggesting a relatively healthy population in an important respect. The share of the nation's income (technically Gross Domestic Product or GDP) spent on health is similar to some of the other countries shown, though more than double the Indian figure and little over half of the United States figure.

The data shown is positive (or provable) but it would be dangerous to leap to generalisations about links between spending and life expectancy. South Africa's lower life expectancy, for example, is influenced by a problem with HIV/AIDS which is less prevalent in the other countries shown. One of the factors contributing to long life expectancy in Japan is a healthier diet and so less obesity.

It is tempting to make the normative statement that everyone should have unlimited treatment as health is so important. However, using resources for health has an opportunity cost and keeping pace with growing demand would be very difficult. Many developed countries have a growing proportion of elderly people. Old people require more health care. Expectations are rising: more people now want cosmetic surgery to improve their appearance, for example. Medical advances make more new and expensive treatments available: Kadcyla, a new drug for breast cancer treatment, costs £90,000 per patient.

Questions

1. What is meant by 'normative statement'? *(2 marks)*

2. Give an example of a positive statement from the above passage, and explain why it is positive. *(4 marks)*

3. Briefly explain one possible reason why new drugs are very expensive. *(4 marks)*

4. Discuss two possible causes of the variations shown in spending on health. *(8 marks)*

5. Assess the opportunity cost of increasing UK health spending to keep up with demand and the trade-offs involved when health spending is limited. *(12 marks)*

Chapter 2

Business objectives

The Joy of Ex Foundation

Sally Beerworth had a successful career in advertising. When her divorce almost cost her her smile, she started writing a funny novel to make herself giggle. As a writer, she started a little Facebook group to help people to smile more. The popularity of the page led to Sally creating postcards and tote bags with her slogans, leading to sales of over £130k in the first year of trading.

Sally was in the awkward position that more people wanted Joy of Ex merchandise than she could afford to print; her biggest challenge has always been financing production to meet the demand. She started out with £1,100 to her name. A Creative Industry Finance Loan and a Small Business Loan helped to finance expansion. Growth of the business means that Joy of Ex now supplies to stores and galleries in the UK, USA, Australia, New Zealand, Sweden, Spain, Canada, Singapore, Dubai, France and Brazil.

Sally now puts aside a chunk of the money she earns, to try to help people financially when they are going through a break up; either by making people smile or by being able to pay for some legal fees or counselling on their behalf. "I wanted to make sure that no one going through a break up ends up snorkelling in vodka or cake mix" said Sally. "I get emails every week from people thanking me for making them smile. What could be better?"

Discussion points

1. What does this information suggest about Sally Beerworth's business objectives?
2. What obstacles hold many people back from starting their own business?
3. Are the objectives of a very large business likely to differ from those of a small business?

Profit maximisation

Incomes

We enjoy eating, having a home and spending money in many, many ways. This makes having an income important to us. If we are employed, we have the security of regular payments from our employer. Once we've had a job for two years, employment law protects us from unfair dismissal and entitles us to compensation if we are made redundant.

Those who have abilities, skills or experience which are valuable to an employer can earn enough to finance a very comfortable life. At the other end of the income scale the UK has millions of employees on low pay, low enough to be classified as living in poverty. To many people, even a relatively low income can be more attractive than the risks and uncertain rewards in starting a business.

Profit

Some **entrepreneurs** who set up businesses are motivated by a desire to get rich, as rich as possible. This can be because riches fund a luxurious material lifestyle or simply because some people define success in terms of wealth. **Profit** provides some security and may be the route to riches for an entrepreneur, provided the total revenue from sales is greater than the total costs of the business.

Inequality

Income inequality is a fact of life and has increased over recent decades. The top 1% of current UK annual incomes average around £250,000 whereas the lowest 1% get an average of £8,000. The top 10% take around one third of all income (ONS 2014 data). The desire to be amongst the top earners is strong in some people. Keeping the rewards of your own ideas and efforts, and making as much as possible, can motivate people to run their own business.

Sales maximisation

Competition

An alternative objective is to maximise sales or sales revenue. A small business may be seen as fragile and risky, whereas growth can bring some stability and increase the chances of survival. Building up a customer base and earning their loyalty can make the future less insecure, for example. A larger business might also have a stronger competitive position, becoming more powerful in their market. The leading UK supermarkets came to dominate the grocery market, with Tesco recording a third of all sales. Customer loyalty and buying power with suppliers made them strong. However, the rise of Aldi and Lidl showed that even strong businesses can still face stiff competition. **Sales maximisation** can sometimes be a short-term objective; once a business has a good **market share** the emphasis could shift to profitability.

Costs

> ### ⚠ WATCH OUT!
>
> Stay clear on the difference between sales revenue and profit. Sales revenue is (price x quantity), the money received from sales; profit is what is left once costs have been deducted.

Satisficing

People are complicated. They have mixed ambitions and their ideas evolve over time. Sally Beerworth gets income from Joy of Ex, but also wants to giggle sometimes and to help others financially. Many entrepreneurs want to have family time and pursue hobbies, rather than spend every minute working. Realistically, 'enough' income often means less than maximum profit. This objective is referred to as **satisficing**. For many students, the idea of doing well enough rather than reaching peak performance will be familiar. Many people face a difficult trade-off between working longer hours to earn more and going home to relax.

Self-employment

The recent UK recession saw many people turn to self-employment and start their own business. The evidence is that many of them earn less from this than they did in employment. Some of these people may be desperate to earn more; others are content with the work-life balance they have.

> **Profit** is a surplus of sales revenue over costs; **profit maximisation** is a possible business objective. It may be a short- or a long-term objective.
>
> **Entrepreneurs** are individuals who set up in business, accepting the risks involved, taking the decisions about what to produce and how, and working out how to market the product.
>
> **Sales maximisation** is an alternative objective, for either the short or the long term.
>
> **Satisficing** means reaching a good enough profit level, without maximising.

Other objectives

Some entrepreneurs derive satisfaction from the **survival** of their business, either because it represents their personal achievement or because it continues a family tradition. Survival grows more important when times are tough.

> **Example**
> Changing market and weather conditions make farming subject to many ups and downs. Many farmers put survival high on their list of objectives and tolerate low incomes in poor years. Leaving the farm, rather than handing it on to the next generation, would be seen by some as failure.

Think!
How much do you and your family value continuity in your lives?

Market share

Building and retaining **market share** has a high priority for some people and can become an objective rather than a means to an end. Market share is the percentage of the total market supplied by any one business. Like sales maximisation, market share can be a short term objective. However, for some businesses it is a permanent priority. Stability and security can be more important than profit, though these objectives can be linked. Leading business owners in a community may value their position as the leading local provider of their product or service.

Sally Beerworth's example showed that businesses need finance, for both capital equipment and work in progress. One important objective is a healthy **return on investment** in the business. This money has an opportunity cost; it could be put to some other use, or kept in the bank, on deposit and earning interest. This becomes particularly important if the business depends on loans. The lenders will expect a return on their money.

Figure 2.1: Business objectives

Efficiency

Operating efficiently with minimum waste and the lowest possible unit costs (cost efficiency) can become a source of pride and satisfaction as well as profit.

Example
Xerox research suggested that 40% of office paper is discarded within a day of being printed; paperless systems cut costs, waste and resource use. Cost efficiency is particularly important when revenue is static or falling and will always contribute to profitability.

Environmentalists concerned with resource depletion and climate change are often passionate about their concerns.

Example
Ecotricity describes its mission as "to change the way electricity is made and used in Britain." Dale Vince, the founder, has structured the business to pay no dividends to shareholders but to reinvest profits in additional green energy production capacity. His declared ambition is to help make Britain "a place in which we all live more sustainable lives and where ethical business is the norm – pursuing outcomes other than profit." His statement reminds us that how and what a business does will have an impact on many groups of people. This example shows how social objectives may influence a firm's decisions.

Social objectives

Social objectives

Ethical policies

Increasingly, businesses are adopting social objectives alongside that of survival. They may recognise the need to make a profit but still not be profit maximisers. They may publicise their ethical policies, which may include concern for **employee welfare**, **customer satisfaction** and the community in which they operate. Many businesses are considering paying a living wage; this is above the national minimum wage and could help to reduce poverty for those in low-paid work.

> **Example**
> John Lewis is a partnership rather than a conventional business. It prides itself on giving value for money, good customer service and treating employees fairly. Survival is certainly important, but not profit maximisation, although the partnership does compete vigorously with other department stores.

Customer satisfaction

For many businesses, maintaining customer satisfaction is simply a matter of ensuring that sales revenues stay healthy. Taking care of customer satisfaction is simply a part of the competitive process, making sure that customers do not switch to other suppliers. But for other businesses, it is a matter of principle that the customer should get a good quality product that meets their needs.

Business objectives

> One possible objective is **survival**, keeping the business going.
>
> **Market share** is the proportion of a specific market that is supplied by one business. It is calculated as total sales by the business as a percentage of total sales in the market. A large share of the market can give the business some market power, a degree of security and reduced risk.
>
> Owners and others who provide finance might prioritise **return on investment**, which would come from interest on loans or dividends for shareholders.
>
> **Cost efficiency** becomes an objective for some businesses because it helps them to compete effectively. Greater efficiency in the use of resources cuts production costs.
>
> **Social objectives** may include **employee welfare**, especially where some employees are likely to be poorly paid. For businesses with environmental concerns, **sustainability** may be an important objective. An **ethical business** takes account of its impact on employees, the local environment and customers; it may have many social objectives.
>
> **Customer satisfaction** can be an objective that ensures repeat purchases, or an outcome of fair and responsible business behaviour that secures a good reputation for the business concerned. It may be pursued in order to ensure good profits or as a matter of principle based on concern for the customer.

Objectives can be based around the personal satisfaction that people in business see as self-fulfilment. This is most evident with creative and artistic businesses such as potters and performers, but it can take many forms. Sally Beerworth, for example, derives satisfaction from making people smile. Many people get fulfilment from doing what they regard as a good and useful job. Other personal objectives can centre on lifestyle. For example, family ties motivate some entrepreneurs to start a business which lets them set their hours to fit in with family commitments. Many people value their social interaction with colleagues. Just being in control of their working life has a strong appeal to some people, who may not want to fit in with conventional employer expectations.

Social objectives

Achieving customer satisfaction may be pursued to achieve good profits or out of concern for the customer.

Exam style question

Suma

Suma is a vegetarian wholefoods wholesaler based in Leeds, specialising in healthy, natural, organic and Fairtrade foods. From modest beginnings 40 years ago, the organisation has moved to bigger premises several times to allow expansion. It now employs around 150 people and has sales revenue of more than £34 million per year. The business was well placed to gain from growing interest in healthy eating. Its approach to business has also proved very successful.

Suma is an equal opportunity, fully democratic workers' cooperative. All the members/employees have the same hourly rate of pay. Members are multi-skilled, bringing flexibility to the business and variety to each person's work. General meetings decide policy and direction. An elected management committee oversees the fulfilment of plans. An emphasis on ethical behaviour and working for sustainability has always been important to Suma.

Questions

1. What is meant by sales revenue? *(2 marks)*

2. Explain what ethical behaviour entails. *(4 marks)*

3. Identify one strength and one weakness of Suma having just one pay rate. *(4 marks)*

4. Discuss the importance of profitability to Suma. *(8 marks)*

5. Assess likely objectives of a workers' cooperative, other than profit. *(12 marks)*

Tyre factory closure

It took Goodyear, a US corporation, more than a year to close a loss making tyre factory in Amiens, France, and to make the 1,173 workers redundant. Early in 2014 the workers took two managers hostage overnight in a campaign for 'enormous' pay-offs.

Maurice Taylor of Titan Tyres (also American) showed interest in taking the factory over and producing specialist tyres on a smaller scale, but after negotiations with unions broke down he described the workers as "lazy, overpaid and talking too much".

Discussion points

1. Why might Titan Tyres have been interested in a loss making factory?
2. Who were the winners and losers from the factory closure?

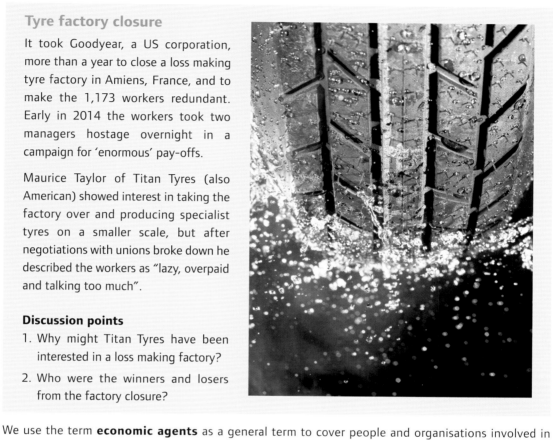

Economic agents

We use the term **economic agents** as a general term to cover people and organisations involved in economic activity. Economic agents may primarily be seen as producers (contributing to output) or consumers (using goods and services). The economic agents with an interest in a specific business are its **stakeholders**. The impact a business can have on its stakeholders will be related to its most fundamental objectives. However, different stakeholders are likely to have different objectives and there can be a trade-off between their interests.

Stakeholders

In a small business the owner is normally the main decision taker and is able to set the objectives. This can be profit maximisation, but a range of alternative priorities was identified in Chapter 2. In a bigger business, the owners are likely to be **shareholders** while the managers are senior employees. Whilst owners are most likely to be interested in profits, professional managers might be more interested in their own salaries or other personal objectives.

Shareholders

Owners, employees and customers are sometimes called primary stakeholders because they have the most direct interest in the business. Each stakeholder group has its own specific concerns. Conflicts between the interests of different stakeholder groups are common and can be complicated.

> The term **economic agents** includes all those groups of people and organisations that are involved in economic activity and take decisions that affect how resources are used.
>
> Anyone with an interest in a business, or feeling an impact from it, is a **stakeholder** in that business.
>
> **Shareholders** are the legal owners of a business. They may have helped to set up the business or they may have bought shares on the stock exchange.

Figure 3.1: Stakeholders

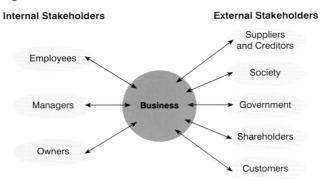

Employees

All the employees of a business are stakeholders. Many businesses describe their employees as their biggest asset and they are often the biggest production cost. There are many examples of businesses that make employee welfare a high priority and reckon that this is just best practice in business, an important element in their success.

Employee welfare

Some businesses are owned by their employees and run to provide jobs and incomes. The John Lewis Partnership (department stores and Waitrose supermarkets) in the UK, with 91,000 employees, is owned by its employees and run to provide jobs and incomes.	At the opposite end of the scale, tensions between employers and employees may hit the headlines, as happened in Amiens. Employers may improve cost effectiveness by cutting jobs, wages, security or pensions; employees may feel that they are being exploited rather than considered.

Owners and shareholders

The owner(s) of the business may be entrepreneur(s) who set up the business and run it, taking all significant decisions. Or there may be a number of owners – shareholders – who have contributed finance for a start-up, or who have bought shares in a well established company. Decisions will be related to business objectives.

Customers

Customer satisfaction

The customers of a business are significant stakeholders. A business that ignores the interests of customers is likely to face falling levels of demand and profitability. It is important to keep customers satisfied.	Some customers have more choice than others as to where and what they buy. The best value products may be too expensive for some and then they need the protection of the law to ensure that the product is 'fit for purpose'.

Suppliers and creditors

Profit and market power

Suppliers of parts or materials have a shared interest in the growth and success of a business. New and small businesses are often given generous terms (such as delayed payment) by suppliers keen to work with them.	Many suppliers are also 'creditors', owed money by the business. Large businesses with market power can use their strength to squeeze down prices paid to suppliers. Farmers have accused the major supermarkets of doing this. Profit seeking businesses want to minimise costs.

The local community, society, the environment and the government

Looking beyond the locality, businesses make a contribution to the wellbeing of the nation with their output, their employment and the taxes they pay to help fund the public sector. They can also be responsible for a contribution to environmental problems. Both legislation and ethical objectives can control harmful aspects of business activity.

Environmental issues

The immediate community around a business has a stake in its success, as a provider of jobs and of incomes which are then spent in the area. Businesses are often valued by the local community.

On the other hand, people may have concerns about the impact of a business. Early in 2015 a £500m waste incinerator at Javelin Park near Gloucester, intended to burn 190,000 tons of waste a year, won planning approval despite strong local opposition due to concerns about noise, traffic and smells.

Find out

Look for three examples of tensions that may arise between different stakeholder groups, each within a specific business. Explain the nature of the possible tensions.

Suppliers are firms from which the business can buy the material inputs or services that are needed in the production process.

Creditors (who may also be suppliers) are those to whom the business owes some money.

Corporate social responsibility

Ethical issues

Amazon

In 2014, internet retail giant Amazon faced claims of tax avoidance. Its accounts showed more than £11 billion routed through the Luxembourg-based arm of the company in 2013 – yet it paid only £4 million in UK corporation tax in the year. In order to reduce its UK tax bill, when customers order goods from Amazon.co.uk, the payment is channelled through the Luxembourg subsidiary, which then pays the UK branch a fee for delivery. The strategy is legal in the UK but Amazon has faced fierce criticism from rival retailers, politicians and consumers over the amount it pays to HM Revenue & Customs. The EU commission says these 'cosmetic' tax arrangements may give Amazon an illegal advantage over its competitors.

Discussion points

1. Why would many people object to Amazon's legal tax avoidance strategy?
2. There have been media reports of Amazon making employees work very hard (perhaps dangerously so) for very low pay. What does the evidence suggest about Amazon's likely business objectives?

Society relies on successful businesses to provide incomes for employees and prosperity for the economy. Amazon is successful, no question. So what is the problem?

Most of us have some ethical values. They will vary a good deal from one person to another, but there is a degree of consensus – there has to be in a civilised society where the rule of law protects us all from various dangers. For example, fairness and integrity are ethical concepts that appeal to many of us and help us to decide how our society should be. (Of course normative statements will appear frequently in the debates.)

Through the media, we encounter ethical issues all the time. Questions relating to business ethics come up whenever an individual or a business is felt to have contravened a fundamental moral principle, a matter of right and wrong. **Corporate social responsibility** in business is all about taking decisions in ways that respect the interests of stakeholders.

Corporate social responsibility (**CSR**) involves a business in behaving in an ethical way and accepting responsibility for its effects on all its stakeholders, including the wider community and the environment.

In recent decades CSR has become an increasingly important consideration for many businesses. Broadly, we can identify three distinct points of view on this:

Ethical responses

- Many successful business owners want to take account of the interests of all their stakeholders, including customers, employees and the wider community. They want to act in a way that shows they care about the well-being of all three, as well as the survival of the business. Ecotricity and Dale Vince offer a good example of this approach.

Reputation

- Other successful businesses have a deep concern for their reputation. They want to be seen to be doing the right things. Reputation is hugely important in terms of the perceived quality of the product and its value for money. Many businesses also want a good reputation as employers: this will help them to recruit the best people. These concerns may lead a business to adopt a strong CSR policy that in reality is primarily focused on profit.

Profit maximisation

- American economist Milton Friedman wrote in 1970 that "business properly has but one goal: to maximise profits." Friedman saw this as the best way to achieve long-term prosperity. When prosperity is the main objective, governments must pursue specific objectives (e.g. consumer protection) by passing the necessary laws. However, advocates of free enterprise argue that too many laws and regulations can stifle business and so damage prosperity.

Show your understanding
The Co-operative Group sets out to be amongst the most responsible businesses and says that *"The Co-operative has always had a purpose beyond profit, and recognises that some things are plainly unjust and need to be tackled, with or without a business case."* Unfortunately, problems with The Co-operative Bank forced the Group to focus more than previously on profitability and survival. Struggling businesses find it harder to look beyond their narrow internal interests.

How does the Co-op stand in relation to the three points of view set out above?

CSR covers a huge range of issues. Consumers expect reliable products. Employees (including managers) expect decent working conditions and pay. Suppliers and creditors expect to be paid on time. Local communities expect freedom from pollution, congestion and noise. Governments expect to be able to collect the taxes that will pay for public services. Shareholders expect generous dividends as a return on their investment.

Dilemmas arise when what is profitable is not necessarily what is most responsible. Short term profit maximisation can work against the interests of wider responsibility and perhaps against the long term interests of the business too.

Tax avoidance: responsibility to the government or the shareholders?

Taxation

Tax evasion means cheating to avoid tax and is illegal, often bringing severe penalties. **Tax avoidance** means structuring business and accounts to legally minimise tax to be paid. Though legal, this can be taken to lengths seen by many as unethical and irresponsible. Both evasion and avoidance leave public authorities poorer and other taxpayers contributing more. **Transnational** or **multinational businesses** operate in many countries and this increases opportunities for tax avoidance.

Politician Margaret Hodge suggested that Amazon should be boycotted because of its tax avoidance history. Amazon said: "[We pay] all applicable taxes in every jurisdiction [where we operate]. We have a single European headquarters in Luxembourg with hundreds of employees to manage this complex operation."

> **Tax evasion** means illegally failing to pay taxes that are due.
>
> Finding legal ways to reduce tax liability is **tax avoidance**.
>
> **Transnational** or **multinational corporations** (**TNC**s or **MNC**s) are businesses with operations in more than one country. Some TNCs are effectively global.

Zero-hours contracts: responsibility to the shareholders or the employees?

The retailer Sports Direct has 20,000 of its 23,000 workforce on zero-hours contracts. Pub chain JD Wetherspoon has 80% of its staff on zero-hours contracts. An ONS survey in 2014 estimated that there are 1.4 million employment contracts in the UK with no guaranteed number of hours. (This does not involve 1.4 million people as individuals can have more than one contract.)

Labour markets

> **Zero-hours contracts** mean that employees work only when they are needed, often at short notice. Their pay depends on hours worked. Some contracts oblige workers to take shifts that are offered, others don't.

The Trades Unions Congress (TUC) sees such contracts as a sign of an increasingly unfair, two-tier workforce in the UK, with those involved in 'precarious labour' penalised in pay and working rights. The table below shows that the balance of advantages with these contracts certainly favours the employer. How responsible and ethical these contracts are is a matter of judgement.

Advantages and disadvantages of zero-hours contracts

Advantages	Disadvantages
To the employer: Flexibility to respond to fluctuating demand for their product. Less costly employment rights for workers.	*To the employer:* Workers possibly less committed and motivated.
To the employee: Some employees value the flexibility.	*To the employee:* Less income. 2014 average £188 per week, nearly £300 below full-time (TUC data). Little financial stability and security, and e.g. hard to get credit cards or mortgages. Fewer rights, e.g. to maternity pay, sick pay or redundancy.

Corporate image

Amazon's Code of Business Conduct and Ethics starts with the statement that "Amazon.com employees should always act lawfully, ethically and in the best interests of Amazon.com." The Sports Direct

Incorporated website says "Corporate responsibility is central to our vision to be an industry leader. Our established corporate responsibility framework focuses on five key areas: employees, health and safety, the environment, our customers, and the community." Many large businesses make similar statements. However, what they say sometimes seems to contrast with what they do.

Image or commitment?

There can be various interpretations of what is responsible and ethical. Some businesses think that CSR is simply good practice, and as such, will lead to profit maximisation in the long run. Other firms may be relatively relaxed about implementing CSR but are very concerned to maintain a positive public image. They have observed that mishaps, like oil spills, bird flu at a turkey farm, stories about child labour, or unreliable products, can damage their reputations seriously. They want their brands to be associated in consumers' minds with good quality and concern for others. They are concerned to emphasise their responsible approach. So it is possible that public statements might not always be a reflection of underlying responsibility and may need to be interpreted very carefully.

Exam style question

Primark

Primark is a retail chain, owned by Associated British Foods (ABF), with over 200 stores across Ireland, the UK, Spain, Netherlands, Germany, Belgium, and Portugal. It employs approximately 50,000 people. Primark mainly sells clothes at the budget end of the market. Its success is based on sourcing cheaply from 600 suppliers in 16 countries. Costs are kept down by making clothes with simple designs and fabrics, only making them in the most popular sizes, and buying stock in huge bulk. Also, in order to maintain value/low prices, Primark try to keep sales volumes high, advertising minimal, and production costs efficient. Sales were up 16% to £4.95bn, and operating profit up 29% at £662m in the year to September 2014.

A problem arose 10 years ago, when Primark scored the lowest of all leading clothing chains in the UK (3.5 out of 20) on the Ethical Index, which ranks criteria such as worker's rights and whether they conduct business with oppressive regimes. They were heavily criticised for having weak business ethics. More recent events have again brought negative publicity. In spring 2013, a Bangladeshi building collapsed and hundreds of people were killed. Primark was one of the retailers buying from garment factories in the building.

In summer 2014 there were protests outside a new store in Berlin. The company recently came under fire when a shopper found a 'cry for help' note hidden inside a pair of Primark trousers. The note spoke of prison inmates in China having to work for Primark like oxen while they were given food that would be considered 'unfit for animals'. Experts have not yet established whether the note was genuine.

Primark joined The Ethical Trading Initiative in 2006 and has paid considerable attention to corporate social responsibility and its public image. It has an 11 point code of conduct for dealings with its supply chain stakeholders. The company produces student resources which tell us, for example (edition 15), that "Primark works to ensure ethical sourcing in a number of ways. It has an Ethical Trade Director, whose role is to make sure Primark goods are sourced ethically and who leads a team of ethical managers and executives based in the key sourcing countries."

Adapted from wordpress.com, Huffington Post and Primark websites

Questions

1. What is meant by Corporate Social Responsibility? *(2 marks)*
2. Identify a possible conflict of interest between stakeholder groups in Primark. *(4 marks)*
3. Briefly explain two possible motives for Primark producing student resources. *(4 marks)*
4. Discuss problems in trading ethically with 600 suppliers in 16 countries. *(8 marks)*
5. Assess the importance of Corporate Social Responsibility to Primark. *(12 marks)*

Chapter 4

What do entrepreneurs do?

Some examples

In 1980 people were still using typewriters. During the subsequent decade, almost all typewriters were replaced with computers. It was so much easier to write on a computer where you could copy, paste, delete and insert, not to mention fixing the minor errors. The computer destroyed the typewriter for all practical purposes. But it enabled many millions of people to write up their thoughts and plans, to express themselves and to meet their employers' needs, using up much less time and effort.

Over the past 30 years, small shops have gradually closed down as superstores took more and more of their business. Nasty superstores! Destroying our High Streets! The funny thing is, people seem to like to shop in large supermarkets and out of town superstores. They have certainly made it worth the supermarkets while, so far. There is a gentle drift back towards specialist shops and boutique-type stores but its impact is quite small so far.

Discussion points

1. On your own, think up three inventions or business developments that have had a big impact on people. Talk to others in your group about your examples and theirs. What do they all have in common?

2. What were the factors that motivated the inventors and the entrepreneurs who brought about the changes you are considering?

3. What risks were involved in the changes that took place?

4. What next? Where do you think the next round of creative destruction is leading?

Commercially, computers and supermarkets have been highly successful in business terms. But in fact, new ventures often fail. Take Richard Branson's spaceship, Virgin Galactica. He spent years planning, testing and developing it. Then in late 2014 it crashed, well before any potential customers could try it out; lives were lost and the outlook for space travel suddenly looked much less promising.

Structural change

Was Branson overconfident? Well, yes; the cost of taking on such risks turned out to be very high indeed. But then, if you had said, when Branson produced and sold his first student magazine at the age of 16, that he would later run an airline, railways and an internet service provider (etc. etc.), no one would have believed you.

We are looking here at examples of **creative destruction**, an idea that comes from the work of Joseph Schumpeter in the 1930s. He said, "only those comfortable with creative destruction can call themselves entrepreneurs." Later, in the 1990s, his work was developed further. The concept of creative destruction highlights the way in which creativity leads to new ideas, inventions and products. These may be so superior to existing products that they attract all or most of the customers. In every case the business is relying on **innovation** to capture the market.

New, nimble, businesses spring up to make and market the superior products, while those businesses that made and marketed the older products find that their profits are falling. Eventually they must either close down altogether or move into different markets where they can still make a profit. (Some typewriter producers closed down altogether but others were already producing a range of products, so could simply shift their efforts to producing more of the still popular products.) This process of some products declining in importance while others take their place is also called structural change.

> **Creative destruction** refers to the way in which quality-improving innovations lead to economic growth. Customers switch to new products and old products become obsolete. Innovations that cut costs and eventually, prices, will have the same effect.
>
> **Innovation** involves developing an idea that will generate new or improved products or production techniques.

Economic growth

The end result of course is that some businesses (or parts of them) are destroyed by the new technologies but new, profitable businesses develop in ways that ultimately spur economic growth and improve standards of living. This is the creative aspect of the process.

The superstores were able to cut prices because they could implement highly efficient IT systems that cut the cost of keeping the shelves stacked with the products that customers most wanted. The businesses that were best able to discern customer preferences and meet them at a reasonable cost grew. Those businesses that lost touch with their markets or were too small to compete effectively had falling sales and gradually shrank in both size and number. This is the destruction element.

Risk

Being creative is quite risky. Very early computers had a number of weaknesses. Some of the early pioneers, like IBM, found that in spite of their early advantage, it was hard to compete with newer businesses, like Apple and Dell. There is an old saying amongst entrepreneurs: "be first or be best". Of course risk is present in all business activity but the risks vary in both character and size.

> **Think!**
> What happened to Nokia, the biggest supplier of mobile phones in 2008? What part did Samsung play in the story?

Dynamic markets

The businesses that find themselves threatened with destruction have a range of options. Many will fight back. The competition from new businesses will force them to research and design new or improved products and this is another important aspect of creativity. It means that the newcomers will not have it all their own way; all competing businesses will have to work on product development, matching their products to consumer preferences.

Competition

Business success does not always depend on innovation. Many businesses base their strategies on close observation of their markets. Consumer preferences change over time and not just in response to the availability of new technologies. Equally, businesses that are not nimble enough to react to changing market forces very often have to reduce output and eventually close down.

Adaptation

> **Examples**
> No-frills products are not confined to the Ryanair and easyJet models. Businesses can succeed because they find ways of offering very good value and attract price-sensitive customers. Sports Direct planned to set up 200 low-cost gyms in 2015, with a membership deal of £5 per month. There are already many such gyms in the US, where 20% of all adults are gym members. The corresponding figure for the UK is 12%. Sports Direct expects to be hugely successful.
>
> An older example is Travelodge – clean, decent and very reasonable. Aldi and Lidl are going from strength to strength all over the world. Uber is disrupting the taxi market, by connecting customers to individual drivers and taxis that allow sharing. The taxi unions are furious.

Uber is disrupting the taxi market by connecting customers to individual drivers.

Disrupters

The businesses that manage to initiate change across the market are known as 'disrupters'. Interestingly, Ford USA is disrupting the vehicle market by making its most popular pick-up truck out of aluminium instead of steel. This reduces the weight of the vehicle by 13% and will be helpful in reducing fuel consumption. Ford has had to replace its welding robots with machines that can use screws, glue and laser-welding, involving huge investments with a considerable risk factor. But they may have gained first mover advantage that can generate big profits.

The role of the entrepreneur

Entrepreneurs are the people who have a business idea and proceed to assemble the resources that are needed to create the product. In doing this they are always accepting a degree of risk. They often use their own savings to finance the start-up; they may do well and make a profit, but they may fail and make a loss. In the UK, one in three new businesses fail within the first three years.

Business startups

To get a business startup going, entrepreneurs need to take many decisions. They need a good understanding of their market and a clear idea about how to set up the production process. They find premises, hire employees and install equipment, using appropriate technologies. A few will know that they have to keep prices at a certain level to be sure of selling the product. Others will be less certain and will need a pricing policy. (They may need a business plan that shows exactly how they will operate.)

Example
Sara Griffiths realised that many people need a good cleaner occasionally but not every week. So she set up an agency that employs a number of cleaners; customers can book one or more according to their needs, without having to go to the trouble of interviewing an individual. Sara takes care of recruitment, organisation and bookings, as well as the legal aspects of employment. Good cleaners like to work for her because they have a reasonably secure job and do not have to look for work for themselves. However Sara is not alone – there have been many start-ups in this field so she has to be competitive.

Risk

From society's point of view, entrepreneurs have a crucial role in the economy. They usually create jobs. They have new ideas and create products that are often innovative. Their willingness to take risks helps to create dynamic markets. In this way they play a part in raising standards of living.

Decisions to expand and develop new markets involve further risk. Some entrepreneurs are very good at thinking up new product ideas but not so good at running the business. Sir Stelios Haji-Iannou, who set up easyJet in 1995, was brilliant at coming up with ideas but not really cut out to be a manager. In 2000 the company was floated on the London Stock Exchange and Stelios backed out of the management so that others could take care of day-to-day decisions. He went on to use the easy brand to set up easyCar, easyHotel and easyGym. Watch out for easyFood, his latest creation.

In complete contrast, JCB is still run by its founding family and has become a massive multinational operation, competing successfully in the earth-moving industry with very big businesses like Caterpillar of the US.

Find out

Think about a small business that you already know a bit about. It could be a local shop or service provider, perhaps an independent hairdresser. Find out anything you can about the entrepreneur behind the business, and work out what they had to do to get the business going.

The great economist John Maynard Keynes wrote about the key features of entrepreneurs, their urge to create a business and their willingness to grasp opportunities that other would find too risky. He said *"If the animal spirits are dimmed and the spontaneous optimism falters, leaving us to depend on nothing but a mathematical expectation, enterprise will fade and die."*

Adding value

Adding value

Entrepreneurs have to be good at **adding value**. Their future depends on their offering value for money; they have to work out how they will create and add value to the product, so that they can sell it at a profit.

Most businesses need some inputs; McCain's chips depend on the business being able to get a supply of potatoes. Inputs may be raw materials but they may also be manufactured items, as with the hairdresser who needs to buy shampoo. These inputs generate costs of production that the business must pay for.

Added value refers to what the business does with the inputs described, in order to make the product worth buying. McCain's process and package the potatoes in such a way that it is really easy for the customer to prepare their chips. For this they pay much more than the cost of the potatoes. Businesses often try to add extra value by adding to the features of the product.

> **Added value** represents the difference between the cost of material inputs and the eventual value of the product in terms of the price that can be charged for it.

Examples

Car manufacturers buy all sort of inputs – sheet metal from the steelworks, and components of all kinds that they get from independent suppliers. Their employees assemble all the bits and pieces on an assembly line which was built on land that the business acquired to create space for the factory. The manufacturers might increase the value added by hiring more and better designers and engineers who can find ways to enhance product features like better locking devices or lower fuel consumption.

No-frills airlines have added value by offering priority boarding, for which they charge extra.

Supermarkets add value by stocking a wide range of products so that much of the time, customers can get everything they need in one place.

Figure 4.1: Adding value in the supermarket

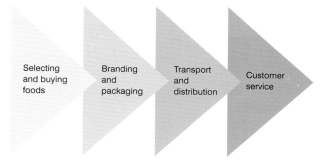

Selecting and buying foods → Branding and packaging → Transport and distribution → Customer service

Think

That small business that you were thinking about earlier, how does it add value to its products? How does it decide what prices to charge to customers?

Exam style question

Magic Inspired Ltd.

Entrepreneur Pete Shepherd set up his advertising agency 'Magic Inspired' in 2006. He had experience of advertising work and good technological skills. He persuaded some friends working in advertising to do freelance work for him. He ran the business from home.

Results were promising and orders came in. Freelance fees are high and after a year, Pete realised that he would be better off recruiting full time staff and using fewer freelancers. He rented a basement office. With three full timers he could pitch ideas to potential customers. He was making a living and paying the staff enough to keep them from going elsewhere. Profits were quite low and were mainly being ploughed back into the business.

By 2009 Pete felt ready to expand again. He needed more specialists to expand his range of advertising media. By this time the sales revenue was just under £500,000 p.a. He got a bank loan to expand, using his own home as collateral.

The next two years were good. Sales grew and Pete felt ready to expand again. He rented a bigger office and recruited a number of very capable employees. By 2011 sales revenue had increased to £900,000 and staff numbers were up to ten. The future looked good.

In 2012 problems became apparent. Some of the bright new staff had required higher pay to join the workforce. Sales were still growing but costs were growing even faster. The business was beginning to make losses. Pete took action. He found a larger business to take over the profitable parts of Magic and some of the staff. He closed down the rest of the business and paid off the debts before the losses grew any further.

Questions

1. What is meant by the term 'entrepreneur'? *(2 marks)*

2. Identify examples of creative destruction in advertising. *(4 marks)*

3. Explain one reason why small businesses such as Magic Inspired sometimes find expansion attractive. *(4 marks)*

4. Examine Pete's attitude to risk. *(8 marks)*

5. Assess the ability of advertising agencies to add value. *(12 marks)*

Chapter 5

Why start a business – and how?

Horticulture

Frank Taylor used to grow chrysanthemums in glass houses. He had a crafty system that could heat and light his glass houses so that the plants thought it was summer when it wasn't, or use blackout to put the plants in darkness, fooling them into producing flowers all year round. For a long time he made a reasonable living from this. Then many Dutch growers invested in bigger glasshouses and used their low-cost North Sea gas to heat them so they could grow flowers more cheaply. Frank couldn't match their prices and had to close down his business. He put the glasshouses on the market and eventually sold them at a rather low price to Peter Thomas, who had an idea he thought might work.

Peter wanted to grow high quality herbs and vegetables both in and out of season and supply them to high-class restaurants and smart food halls like Harrods and Selfridges in London's West End. Eight years after starting he is making a living. If he can find a few more customers he can expand because he isn't yet using all the space he has.

Discussion points

1. Peter isn't making a profit but he is covering all his costs.

2. How might he be feeling about this?

3. What might he be able to do to change his situation? Could he be motivated by the incentive to expand?

Covering costs

Every business has to cover its overall costs in the long run. If it does not, it will make losses, accumulate debts and will soon have to close down. No matter what the objectives of the entrepreneur may be, the marketplace is actually very brutal and people in business cannot afford to make losses for long.

Revenue, costs and profit

First they must cover all of their costs so they can pay the employees, the rent and the costs of other inputs. But business is often risky. Entrepreneurs usually **invest** their own money in their businesses, not to mention a great deal of time. They need to be rewarded in the form of income for their own needs and compensation for the risks they are taking. A key question for them will be how much **profit** they can make, initially just to make a living. If they want to expand, profits will have to contribute to the costs of future expansion. Profit is the difference between **sales revenue** and **costs of production**. In the case study above, Frank was covering all his costs. But if he was actually to make a profit he needed to expand and find new markets.

The prospect of profit provides an **incentive** to go to all the trouble of setting up a business, or expanding an existing one. The higher the price that can be charged, the greater the incentive to supply the product. Often, entrepreneurs are comparing possibilities, looking to decide which product offers the best incentive.

Costs of production are all the payments that have to be made in order to get a product into the market place. They will include wages, premises and all other input costs – raw materials, components, inputs bought from wholesalers, business rates, interest, energy bills and so on.

sales revenue = price x quantity sold

profit = sales revenue – costs of production

Investment means spending now in order to generate income in the future, i.e. investing in premises, capital equipment (such as machinery, computers or vans), researching and developing the product, and training key employees.

Incentives are financial and other rewards that can induce people to behave in a certain way. The prospect of profit acts as an incentive that encourages businesses to produce more or to develop a new or different product.

Entrepreneurs and the incentive of profit

Innovation

Chapter 2 looked in detail at profit maximisation and sales maximisation. There is no doubt about it, potential profit can be a very big incentive to invest in a start-up or to expand a business. One good way to do this is by coming up with an innovative product. The late Steve Jobs did this with Apple's iPad. Tablet computers had already been invented but they were rather cumbersome and lacked user-friendliness. Effectively, Apple redesigned the product so that it met the needs of a wide range of people.

Example

Apple's philosophy is all about designing products that work really well, look good and appeal to customers. The company has excelled in this and as a result has been able to charge very high prices without losing market share. By the end of 2014 huge profits were accumulating. Clearly, even if high quality design is an important business objective for Apple, profit maximisation is at least equally important. If it were not so, the prices might be lower.

Meeting consumers' needs

When people flock to buy a particular product, they are doing so because it is something they want or have a great need for. So we can look at profit as an incentive from two angles.

● Customers are willing to pay good prices for products they really want.

● The possibility of charging a good price creates prospects of profit for the entrepreneur.

Incentives

It follows that the business that can create a really good product that sells well is going to make a profit. In a capitalist economy, businesses therefore have an incentive to study customer needs and tailor their product to people's preferences. Provided markets are competitive, profit acts as an incentive and as a signalling mechanism that matches output to consumer demand right across the range of products we consume.

Product design and innovation

Getting the product right doesn't have to be as complicated as the development of a new Apple invention. However, using new technologies can create many opportunities for businesses. They may use them to create and supply new products. Or they may produce existing products in a more efficient way, thus reducing costs and perhaps also prices, and increasing sales revenue.

"This is a real technological breakthrough"

How profit works

PROFIT = TOTAL SALES REVENUE – TOTAL COST

Profit is the difference between the total sales revenue and all production costs. The most obvious reason for setting up a business is that all of the profit made belongs to the owner, so the more profit the business makes, the richer the owner will become. There is a clear incentive for the owner to work hard, and a visible link between their effort and their financial reward. Profit is the financial motive for going into business.

The profit motive

If you work for an employer, you are likely to receive a weekly or monthly wage or salary. You might also receive bonuses linked to your performance, or overtime pay if you have worked extra hours, but this isn't always the case. You may or may not feel motivated to work hard.

Successful entrepreneurs tend to be hard-working. They are likely to be motivated by the chance to earn more for their hard work by setting up on their own. Remember, though, that there is also the chance of making no profit at all (or even of making a loss), which is why the entrepreneur must also be willing to take calculated risks.

> **Profit** compensates the entrepreneur for carrying the risks associated with running a business.

Show your understanding

What happens when a new product comes on the market and consumers flock to buy it? Choose a product like this that you have observed selling very well. How did the producer business respond? Was there a time when the product was hard to find because demand had been so strong? What happened to the price of the product? Did other businesses try to copy the product? Did this have any impact on the price? Tell the story in your own words. What role did profit have in the outcome?

Non-financial motives

Most entrepreneurs would be likely to say that profit was not their only motive. Many do greatly value the freedom and independence that self-employment can bring. However, without an employer to take care of the business decisions, the entrepreneur may feel overwhelmed by the risks and uncertainties.

Exploring motivation

Independence suits those entrepreneurs who like to work in their own way. They may value the self-fulfilment and satisfaction that comes from doing the work that they enjoy. Entrepreneurs create a business from nothing so they can feel proud of what they have achieved. They can control their own work and decide which activities they want to focus on. There is scope for creativity; the work may involve product design or a creative approach to the process of production.

Working from home suits many people who would rather not have to travel each day to a workplace. It can be a very cost efficient way to work, making it easier for the business to offer keen prices and compete in the market place. It can be particularly suitable for start-up businesses in that it reduces risk.

Social entrepreneurship is on the increase. Many people want to set up a business that will address difficult social issues. Usually it will be a not-for-profit business. It may depend on donations and grants from government or private sector organisations. Or it may charge for some or all of the services it offers, but plough back the profits into the business in order to develop or expand.

Ethical business is a term that encompasses a huge range of different approaches to business management. The word 'ethics' relates to doing what is 'right'. Social entrepreneurs deliberately set up in business for ethical reasons. Many businesses do set out to behave in an ethical way, seeking to treat all of their stakeholders appropriately while making a profit. Others merely advertise their ethical principles but continue, quietly, to make profit maximisation their primary objective.

What do social entrepreneurs do?

Social objectives

- Social entrepreneurs look for innovative ways of tackling social or environmental problems, either by developing new products or by devising new ways of delivering existing products more effectively.
- They use everyday business strategies and new technologies to develop novel solutions.
- They often aim to create jobs and may look to take on employees who are disadvantaged in some way.
- They may have a deep commitment to alleviating poverty or dealing with specific local problems.
- They mobilise volunteers and help to change attitudes.
- There may be a fine line between a social enterprise and a charity. But both must find a way to cover all of their costs if they are to survive.

Social entrepreneurs use business methods and strategies to achieve social objectives. They seek innovative solutions to difficult social problems.

Example

Smart Savings, located in Cornwall, is a community interest company that offers ethical financial and employment services. It specialises in claims management (helping with financial compensation claims) and personal finance training (for people who have got into debt or need understandable financial advice from a trusted source). It is funded partly by grants and donations but also charges for some services where appropriate. They recently recruited 7 people in the age-range 16-18 to do a cookery course.

What do ethical businesses do?

It has been estimated that over 80% of large UK businesses have an ethical code. This will contain the principles on which the business is run, based on honesty and integrity and the company view of the 'right' way to do business. It gives guidance to professionals who will be taking difficult decisions. Almost all businesses want to be seen to be behaving in an ethical way.

Example

Google Forest Watch is a mapping platform that records data on tree cover loss, helping scientists to monitor the state of global forest cover.

Ethical business

The Ethisphere Institute of Management, a management consulting business, gathers information about ethical businesses and produces a list of 144 most ethical businesses worldwide. A large majority of the companies on the list are from the USA, but the list does include Marks and Spencer, the Northumbrian Water Group and the Ethical Fruit Company Ltd, all based in the UK.

This list also includes Starbucks, which has a long track record of tax avoidance in a range of countries where it operates, and Ford Motor Company, which made big profits from rising sales of high-end gas-guzzling vehicles when oil prices went down in late 2014. Ethisphere's Most Ethical Company in 2014 was H&M, the clothing retailer. Critics say that its analysis did not take into account the working conditions in the factories where the clothes are manufactured.

Find out

Gather information about two of the companies mentioned above and assess the extent to which their policies are genuinely ethical.

Non-financial motives are reasons for setting up in business that are not linked to making a profit.

Ethical motives lie behind firms' efforts to do 'what is right'. For example, a business or organisation may contribute to projects that benefit the local community. Or it may be committed to ethical employment or buy inputs from environmentally sustainable sources.

How do entrepreneurs get started?

Factors of production

However carefully the business objectives have been thought through, any business start-up, and any expansion of the existing business, will require many practical steps, simply to get organised. **Enterprise** entails bringing **factors of production** together to create desirable goods or services. These are the essential inputs to the production process, which fall into three categories, **land**, **labour** and **capital**.

- *Land* means more than just the solid parts of the earth's surface. Of course it includes the space required for the business location but to economists, it is an umbrella term covering all the natural resources that can be found and exploited, from diamond and oil deposits to wind and water. The state of knowledge and technology help determine which land resources are used at any time. (A major concern is that some land resources are used unsustainably, so they may become increasingly scarce and therefore expensive.)

- *Labour* is often the biggest component input. Personal service activities (such as hairdressing) depend very heavily on labour. Many businesses see their labour force as both their biggest cost and their greatest asset. There are currently around 31 million people working (providing labour) in the UK. The biggest trend through the last century was the rise in the proportion of women in paid employment. One of the notable trends of recent years has been a tendency for the gap in incomes between skilled and unskilled workers to widen.

- *Capital* is our name for productive equipment. It includes machines, buildings and infrastructure, such as drains, roads and bridges. An important feature of capital is that it can be used repeatedly rather than just once like a raw material. So, for example, a chef's pots and pans are capital but the vegetables he prepares today are raw material. Building up bigger and technologically better stocks of capital plays a very important role in increasing incomes and wealth everywhere.

Adding value

The entrepreneur must see what is needed and make things happen. Enterprise itself is sometimes called the fourth factor of production, because without it, no business would actually go into production. The factors of production are all part of the business and the combined value of their contribution is the value added by the production process. But the entrepreneur must create a well-organised business and carry the risk.

Risk

In any enterprise there is someone (or some group) hoping for success, but this is not guaranteed. (A USA study found that 27% of new restaurants fail within a year of opening and that 50% last 3 years or more.) Most businesses hope for profit but some make losses. Entrepreneurs have to look for ways of minimising risk, especially in the critical early stages of their business start-up.

Factors of production are land, labour and capital, the essential inputs into the production process. Together they contribute the value added to the output, which makes it saleable in the market place.

Enterprise is sometimes called the fourth factor of production because it is fundamental to the organisation of the economic activity and willingness to take risks in return for profit.

Labour means human effort contributing to production. Wages and salaries are received in return.

Land means space where production can be located but it also refers to the natural resources that are inputs to the production process. Landowners receive rent.

Capital includes premises and equipment that are used repeatedly in production. Owners of capital receive interest or dividends.

Find out

The spread of the internet has encouraged a wave of enterprise because start-up costs for web businesses are often low; this reduces the amount at risk in a new venture. If you can, identify and speak with someone who has set up a web business, ask them about their motives and their hopes for the future, and also what difficulties and risks they have faced. If you can't find a business of this kind, investigate any willing business that got started in say, the past five years.

Chapter 6

Why do we specialise?

Adam Smith

Long ago – a big idea

Adam Smith, one of the founders of modern economics, published his most famous book, *The Wealth of Nations*, in 1776. In it he described what he saw on a visit to a pin factory.

"One man draws out the wire, another straightens it, a third cuts it, a fourth points it, a fifth grinds it at the top for receiving the head; to make the head requires two or three distinct operations… to whiten the pins is another; it is even a trade by itself to put them into the paper; the important business of making a pin is, in this manner, divided into about eighteen distinct operations, which in some factories, are all performed by distinct hands."

Discussion points

1. One person's output of pins would be very low. Think of as many reasons as you can, why people taking on specific tasks will increase output. Explain your reasons.

2. Think of at least three other industries which will function more efficiently when work is broken down in this way.

3. What kinds of business might not benefit from this approach? Give an example and explain why.

Specialising

Subsistence farmers don't specialise. They have a range of skills and produce what they need to feed themselves. They construct their own homes. They hope to have a surplus of some products so that they can exchange these for simple tools or clothes.

Exchange

There aren't very many subsistence farmers left in the world now, and for very good reasons. Their standard of living is very low indeed. If you imagine yourself stranded on a far-away island you can see at once that you would not have much in the way of consumer goods. We generally rely on **specialisation** and **exchange** to provide all of our needs. Having ways of exchanging what we produce for the other things we need and want is a key factor in improving standards of living. It allows us to specialise in what we do best, so that each of us is maximising efficiency and producing the most we can.

> **Specialisation** means that people make the most of their skills by concentrating their expertise in a particular field. As a skilled person produces more, output per head will rise; across the economy, standards of living will improve.
>
> **Exchange** allows us to trade our own products for those of others, giving us a range of consumer goods and services that we want or need. Money makes the exchange of products easy, enabling us each to specialise and become more skilled and productive.

The division of labour

Adam Smith was observing the division of labour in the pin factory. Of course you can see many ways in which the division of labour can occur. In the Industrial Revolution that followed, increasing numbers of people acquired specialist skills and output grew rapidly. Some individuals came up with innovations, creating new kinds of machinery with increasing sophistication. New skills were developed and this process grew and expanded into the type of economy we have today. The pace of innovation now is as fast as it has ever been.

Specialisation

The division of labour is not just about manufacturing goods. There is just as much specialisation going on in services. Until recently, if you needed a blood test, your doctor might have taken a small sample of your blood. Now, the doctor is likely to send you to the

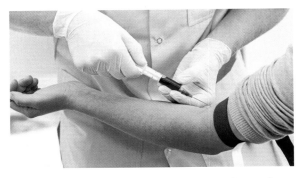

practice nurse, who has all the necessary skills to do this, but will do the job for a lower rate of pay. This is a more efficient way of using scarce resources – the doctor will concentrate on diagnosis and treatment.

> The **division of labour** involves organising employees so that individuals specialise in one part of the production process. As they become quicker and more proficient at specific tasks, output increases. People specialise in the type of work to which they are best suited.

Show your understanding

Identify two other situations where people are becoming more specialised and the division of labour in the workplace is intensifying. Then identify one type of production where people are being encouraged to specialise less and become more versatile, and explain why this is happening in that particular situation.

Sounds boring

Might doing the same thing over and over again get boring? Could someone become careless after a spending a whole day doing blood tests, or attaching the same component to each car that goes past on the assembly line? The answer has to be yes.

Modern production management involves ensuring that each employee has meaningful tasks that can be carried out efficiently. Sometimes mechanising a process takes the boredom out of production – automated equipment and computers will increasingly take care of some of the boring bits of the work and leave people with the interesting jobs where some degree of human judgment may be an advantage.

Service sectors

Modern economies have large service sectors – and these often increase in size as new technologies are introduced. Developed countries (Europe, North America, Japan, Australia) typically have service sectors that employ over 70% of the labour force. We call them mature economies and they are increasing in number. Most service sector production currently requires many people – think of health care, education and local government administration. As job opportunities in manufacturing decline, new jobs are created in the service sector. (Think of restaurants and coffee shops.)

Efficiency

Increasing efficiency

Specialisation and the division of labour give us good ways of increasing efficiency. Increased efficiency reduces production costs; it means using fewer resources in the production process. People take less time to complete their tasks if they are experienced in what they are doing.

> **Efficiency** means using resources in the most economical way possible. As efficiency increases, output per person employed will be higher. Specialising involves acquiring skills and understanding that speed up production processes and may also lead to new or better quality products. Value added may increase as know-how develops.

Strix

Strix is a very specialised company making technologically sophisticated products. It describes itself as a global consumer technology solutions provider.

Intermediate goods

The company started out making control mechanisms in the Isle of Man in 1982. Some of the work is still done there. It was always an innovative business. It developed the technology for cordless kettles. But it does not produce kettles, or any other consumer product: it makes what we call intermediate goods, component parts for a wide range of end products. It is part of a trend whereby relatively small businesses specialise in highly technical devices that are usually hidden inside much larger products, greatly improving their functionality. Intel is the biggest example, manufacturing micro-chips for computers. There are many others and most you will never have heard of.

This approach involves very close collaboration with customers. Strix devises specific new products to meet the needs of leading brand manufacturers like Tefal and Morphy Richards. For kettles, it manufactures tiny sensors that monitor the temperature of the water inside and tell the kettle to switch off when the water is boiling. The sensor protects against boiling dry and contributes to the safety of appliances to which it is fitted. The development process looks like this and involves working with customers in a four-stage process:

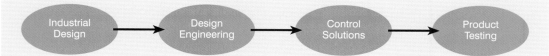

Strix has received a string of Queen's Awards, for Exports, Enterprise Innovation and International Trade. The chief executive says success has come from the company's relentless pursuit of innovation, embedded in its culture. He went on:

Innovation

"We're not resting on our laurels. At Strix there is a constant flow of innovation and we're always seeking new opportunities and global partners." One in five people in the world use Strix safety controls every day.

The business has had about two thirds of the world market in kettle sensors for some time. It has expanded the business by diversifying into the design and manufacturing of components for coffee makers, water filters, and anti-bacterial filter systems. Some of the manufacturing processes take place in China.

Strix attributes its success to the very high quality of the people and the teamwork in its multicultural workforce. It recruits its design engineers and its production managers with the greatest care. But it also pays a lot of attention to the quality of its marketing and customer service teams. The CEO goes on: "we have forged lasting relationships with our valued partners around the globe, and continue to build and strengthen these links as we retain our market-leading position."

Questions

1. What is meant by 'very specialised'? *(2 marks)*

2. Explain how Strix might have developed such a large market. *(4 marks)*

3. Explain why partnership with customers is important to Strix. *(4 marks)*

4. Discuss likely reasons for Strix's share of the kettle sensor market. *(8 marks)*

5. Assess the case for specialising in a tiny component rather than manufacturing complete products for consumers. *(12 marks)*

Chapter 7

How does economic change affect business?

Start here

Jim is an electrician. He worked for other people for some years but then decided to set up his own business. At that point he had to have a van and all the necessary kit for the job. He also needed cash to pay for advertising for customers and something to keep himself going until he had enough customers paying promptly to cover his personal needs. He had savings, enough to cover all of the above except for some of what he needed to pay for the van. He got a bank loan which would last for two years, at a reasonable rate of interest, 6%, and this together with some of his savings meant he could buy the van.

Unfortunately, three months after Jim took out the loan, interest rates rose and the bank asked for 9% in future.

Discussion points

1. What would the rise in interest rates mean for Jim?

2. What other risks might make Jim vulnerable?

3. Under what circumstances might Jim's business venture fail?

Businesses often need to borrow money for any number of reasons, the main ones being:

● When they are just starting up they are likely to need money from the entrepreneur's pocket *and* borrowed money, just to pay for premises and equipment – the capital they need.

● If they want to expand they will need to borrow again, maybe to fund market research, maybe to pay for more capital equipment.

● In both cases, businesses need **working capital** to pay for inputs and wages, ahead of the time when sales revenue comes in.

Interest has to be paid on loans. Lenders will not lend unless they can expect some reward for doing without their money until it is paid back. Rising **interest rates** on business loans increase costs of production. Some businesses can put prices up but some (like Jim) will simply lose customers if they do that. That will mean getting less profit. Low interest rates can make it easier for businesses to set up, or to expand and create jobs. Interest rates vary; they may be higher if the borrower is actually quite risky and may not be able to pay back the lender. But they may also be high because of government policy. When this is the case, businesses can be discouraged from investing.

Interest rates

> **Working capital** refers to the finance needed by a business to cover production costs – rent, wages and the cost of other inputs needed – until payment is received.
>
> **Interest rates** specify the amount that has to be paid by the borrower to the lender. Where there is a risk that the lender will not be repaid, the interest rate will be higher.

Monetary policy

The Bank of England is in charge of controlling inflation, the rate at which prices rise. Mostly, it seeks to influence the rate of inflation by adjusting interest rates. (You will learn much more about this later in the course). So if the data suggest that inflation is accelerating, the Bank may adjust interest rates upwards and this will force all borrowers to pay more for their loans; this will discourage excessive borrowing.

However, you just happen to be living in unusual times. Interest rates have not been behaving normally. Now you need to find out why.

Interesting times

Financial crisis

In 2008-9, a major financial crisis hit the global economy. Put simply, many banks had made risky loans to borrowers. Many borrowers had taken out loans they could not really afford to repay. When unemployment began to rise, some banks found that a number of their mortgage borrowers had stopped repayments. This left them out of pocket and forced them to borrow more money themselves, just to keep going.

As the news got out, confidence in some banks plummeted. People and businesses tried to get their money out of the banks that looked set to fail. As they did this, the banks got into more and more trouble and stopped lending to each other. The financial system froze and many businesses found that demand for their products was sinking.

As a way of getting their economies moving again, most central banks (like the Bank of England) decided to reduce interest rates dramatically, to 0.5% in the UK case. And there they have stood, for years on end – a highly unusual situation. Interest rates would rise in the UK if inflation were to accelerate. But at the time of writing inflation is low and falling. More on this later.

Find out

Base Rate

1. What is the Base Rate of the Bank of England right now?

2. What impact is it likely to be having on business decisions?

The bottom line

- A very low interest rate ought to encourage businesses to invest and expand and create jobs. In practice they will only do this if demand for their product is expected to grow.

Interest rate changes

- Low interest rates do mean that homeowners with mortgages have lower monthly payments to make and this can mean that they have more money to spend on consumer goods and services. If so, some businesses will find demand for their products growing.

- Higher interest rates will have the opposite effects.

The Bank of England.

The impact of exchange rate changes

International trade is important to the UK. In fact, understanding the UK economy is impossible without considering the exchange rate. Figure 7.1 shows that the pound fell by a total of 25% between 2006 and the end of 2008, compared to the currencies of its main trading partners. This meant that if nothing else changed:

● Imports were roughly 25% dearer in late 2008 than in 2006.

● Exports were roughly 25% cheaper in foreign markets. Foreign buyers would find UK products much more competitive than before.

● It was far easier to compete in 2009-10 than it had been in 2006. Exporters were able to sell more in foreign markets and UK businesses found it easier to compete with imports.

Falling exchange rates

Figure 7.1: The UK exchange rate

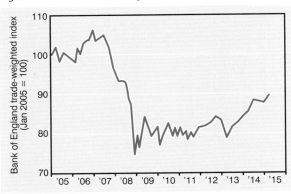

Source: Bank of England

Of course, it takes businesses and consumers time to adapt to new exchange rates. But Figure 7.2 shows that in the two years after the dramatic fall in the UK exchange rate, exports rose by 20%. However, imports really did not change very much. All that can be said is that they rose by a bit less than exports.

Since 2009, the UK exchange rate has been broadly stable. This has helped businesses that export quite considerably, even though it has not led to a fall in imports. These figures are for goods. Typically the UK imports more goods than it exports and the difference is to some extent balanced by high service exports (including financial services).

Figure 7.2: Export and import volumes (goods)

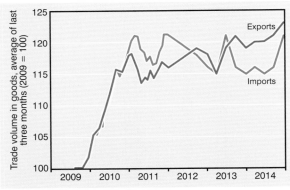

Source: ONS Statistical Bulletin

> The **exchange rate** is the rate at which one currency is exchanged for another. Usually exchange rates change continuously, but by small amounts. An economy that is struggling to compete is likely to find its exchange rate falling.

Index numbers

You will notice that both Figures 7.1 and 7.2 use index numbers. These show the amount of growth (or decline) relative to a particular year – if you subtract 100 from the total you get the percentage change. (You will learn more about this handy way of measuring change later.)

⚠ WATCH OUT!

Figure 7.1 uses the exchange rate index to measure the change in the currencies of the UK's main trading partners as a group. The value of 100 was given for the base year, 2009, so it is easy to see the percentage change. You do not need a deep understanding of this process but you must be able to interpret the figures correctly, i.e. spot the percentage change.

Oil prices and exchange rates

Example

Diageo is the world's biggest distiller. Amongst its biggest sellers are Smirnoff vodka, Johnny Walker whisky and Guinness beer. But in early 2015 they announced a fall in their profits. The chain of events went like this. In 2014 oil prices fell. Big oil and gas exporters like Russia, Venezuela and Nigeria were getting less cash from their exports so their exchange rates fell sharply. This pushed up the price of imports and led to a sharp fall in Diageo's sales in those countries. The more an economy can export, the more foreign currency it can spend on imports and vice versa.

Taxation (and government spending)

Tax increases cut consumer spending power. This applies to **income tax** and some other taxes too. So when taxes are rising, consumer spending falls and businesses supplying consumer products will face falling sales and reduced profits, and vice versa.

> **Income tax** is levied on the incomes of individuals. There is a personal allowance which is tax free, which is generally increased by at least the rate of inflation, in the Budget each year.

Government expenditure cuts have similar effects. If the government cuts welfare payments, or teachers' pay, the recipients have less to spend and some businesses will notice the falling sales and profits. The affected businesses will:

Taxing, spending and business

- Reduce output.
- Put off investing in new equipment.
- Not replace employees who leave.
- Reduce their training schemes.
- Perhaps, make some employees redundant.

All these consequences will have knock-on effects on businesses. The more employees are made redundant, the more consumer spending will be likely to fall. If investment falls, businesses involved in construction or manufacturing equipment will cut output, repeating the same process.

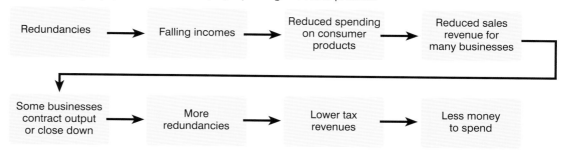

Spending more on community care

As fewer and fewer people stay in hospital for a long time, care in the community has expanded. Governments are spending more on community care, partly to keep NHS costs down and partly to care better for the ageing population. Most of this community care is actually provided by small businesses. They usually call themselves care agencies; they can be not-for-profit organisations or, simply, businesses.

Money spent on community care comes partly from tax revenue. Expenditure cuts in this area will reduce the agencies' revenue and profits.

Question

How would falling revenue affect a care agency? What would actually happen if demand decreases?

Tax – the business view

Corporation tax takes a certain percentage of annual profits. Besides corporation tax, businesses pay Business Rates – to their local authorities. These can be a hefty expense and add to their costs. Essentially business rates are just another tax. Arguably they pay for local authority services, but not all entrepreneurs see it that way.

Business taxes

> **Example**
> Many of the shop owners and cafés in South Road have been angry about their business rates. Almost all are small businesses, with just the one outlet. Maria's World of Cakes specialises in cakes for celebrations – their adverts say "Our only limit is your imagination." They had to pay £4,850 to the Council. This is enough to make a big dent in profits. Maria said "The amount of money we have to pay in business rates is not fair."

Value Added Tax (**VAT**) is paid on sales of all consumer products except for food eaten at home, housing, books and newspapers and public transport (with a few exceptions). In late 2008 it was reduced from 17.5% to 15%, to give people a bit more spending power and lift the economy generally. In January 2010 it went back up to 17.5%. When VAT rises, most retailers put the price up to cover the extra tax. But not quite all do. Just a few will hold the price to keep the competition away. As of 2012, VAT was raised to 20%. The same applies to other sales taxes, like alcohol duty.

Euston Road, London, soon after Budget Day, 2009

> **Corporation tax** is paid by businesses; the level will be a percentage of the profit made. For businesses making less than £300,000 profit in a year, it is currently 20%. Higher profits are taxed at 21%.
>
> **VAT**, value added tax, is collected by businesses and takes 20% of the value of the sales, less the cost of all the inputs bought from other businesses.

From the business point of view, an increase in VAT puts up prices and reduces customers' spending power. If the product is something customers can manage without, sales revenue will fall. VAT also creates an administrative burden on the business. In general business communities tend to favour tax cuts and dislike tax increases because of the effect on demand across the economy.

> **Think**
> Would you expect consumers to have the same attitude to taxes that people in business have? When you have drawn your conclusion, provide at least two reasons for your view.

Unemployment

Falling spending

People who lose their jobs typically lose income as well. They have to cut back on spending and do without some of the consumer products they used to buy. We have already seen that this will lead to some businesses' facing a lower level of demand for their products. The knock-on effects of cutting output and making employees redundant can lead to a downward spiral and slow growth or a shrinking economy.

Unemployment

In the UK, unemployment rose substantially after the financial crisis but not as much as it did in many other similar economies (or as much as it had in the 1980s and 90s in the UK). Many businesses held on to their most skilled and valued employees for as long as they possibly could. They cut their pay and sometimes their hours too, because they were facing falling demand from customers. But clearly, employers wanted to keep people with valued skills. Employees put up with the reduced incomes because it was better than being made redundant and depending on unemployment benefits.

Figure 7.3: UK unemployment, LFS, 1973-2014

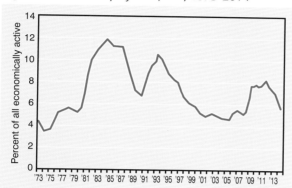

Source: ONS

When unemployment gets low, it is harder for employers to recruit new employees. Some may find better jobs elsewhere; this is a clear indication that if they want to keep valued employees, the employers must think about pay rises. Attracting new staff will mean offering better pay too.

Skills: December 2014

Business leaders became seriously worried about chronic skill shortages in the UK, which looked set to reduce efficiency and to slow the process of economic recovery.

Kevin Green, chief executive of the Recruitment and Employment Confederation (REC), said:

> *"Last year we had nine areas of skills shortages, now we have 43 areas. Every single type of engineering is in short supply, from mechanical to software, civil to electrical. In IT, coders, programmers and developers are all in short supply; there's a shortage of doctors and nurses in the National Health Service; and we need about 20,000 more teachers in the UK. The situation's been getting worse for the last 18 months."*

The employers organisation, the CBI, agreed. They said:

> *"Our most recent survey shows that skills shortages are becoming more acute. This is particularly true for high-level skills in sectors like engineering, technology, digital, manufacturing and construction."*

The Business Secretary, Vince Cable, said that the UK's skills gap is "crippling" the country's manufacturing sector.

Discussion point

Some skill shortages are worldwide. What measures might be required to deal with the problem?

Skill shortages

Skill shortages have been around for a long time. But when businesses were struggling after the financial crisis, some people with scarce skills moved to other jobs and now it is not so easy to get them back and many businesses are finding it difficult to recruit. Such shortages will be less noticeable when unemployment is higher as employers will stand some chance of finding people who have been made redundant elsewhere.

You might think that employers would consider putting more money and effort into training schemes. Successive governments have had the same idea. But training is expensive and both sides seem to hope that the other will take action. Neither governments nor businesses come out of this well, despite recent efforts to increase the number of apprenticeships.

> **Skill shortages** occur when the people available for work do not have the skills that employers are seeking. This is particularly likely to happen when the economy is growing, unemployment is relatively low and new technologies are being widely adopted.

The impact of unemployment on work habits

Loss of skills

Long-term unemployment typically has a bad effect on work habits. People who are not using their skills may lose some of them. They may become unaccustomed to the demands of the workplace and have difficulty settling into a new job when vacancies finally appear. This has clear implications for employers.

Inflation

Effects of inflation

Inflation means a general rise in prices. Figure 7.4 shows that it was not too much of a problem in the period after 2013. But when inflation is accelerating it creates problems for businesses, including:

● Uncertainty – businesses need to be able to plan ahead. Inflation can cause some instability in the economy and that makes planning harder, e.g. if they are considering whether to expand or to branch out into new product areas.

● Demands for pay increase – unless pay keeps pace with prices, most employees will be unhappy.

● Imports from economies with lower rates of inflation may make it hard for some businesses to compete.

All this means that most governments want to avoid accelerating inflation if at all possible.

Figure 7.4: UK Inflation rates, 1978-2014

Inflation

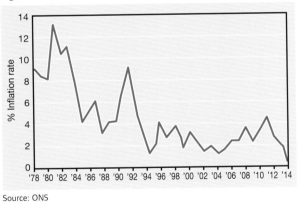

Source: ONS

Many EU economies are at the time of writing headed towards deflation, i.e. a generalised fall in prices. This frightens governments and economists because if people believe prices are falling, they may delay major purchases. This will be really bad news for many businesses; the economy could slow down disastrously. So policy makers try to keep inflation rates around 2%.

Find out

Find out what happened to the inflation rate from 2015 onwards. Find data that will help you to update each of the Figures 7.1-7.3 as well. Outline the most pressing economic problems in the news now. What different policy approaches have you read about?

Exam style questions

1. Assess the impact of a falling exchange rate on the UK economy in general and on businesses in particular. *(8 marks)*

2. A new government has promised to increase spending and cut taxes on fuel. Evaluate the likely effects on businesses and individuals. *(12 marks)*

Demand

However well an entrepreneur organises production, a business will fail unless it can attract customers. When people make choices on what to do with their limited incomes, they have many alternatives. It is not enough that people admire or even want the product; what matters is whether or not they will buy it. Demand is our name for the human wish to obtain goods and services. **Effective demand** means willing- ness to buy along with ability to pay.

Choice

As incomes are limited, any spending choice has an opportunity cost. A logical (or 'rational') consumer should make choices bringing the highest possible satisfaction from the available income. In reality, we don't always make rational choices. Behavioural economists have studied how and why we make less than perfect choices. We know within ourselves that our choices are not always good. However, it is reasonable to start by saying that consumption brings satisfaction or 'welfare' and that we want more satisfaction rather than less.

The spending opportunities that attract are those that we value the most; otherwise we shouldn't choose them. Because we want things enough to pay for them, businesses can earn sales revenue by supplying them. This suggests that consumers ultimately decide what will be produced, and in the process how resources will be used. Market forces, which involve consumer demand interacting with producers' supply, leads to an allocation of resources that gives us the best selection of goods and services obtainable from existing resources. This is called **consumer sovereignty**.

Consumer sovereignty

In the real world, consumer sovereignty has its limitations. For example, it depends on markets being competitive. If clever advertising creates desire for a product, this shows that some power really rests with businesses. Fashion trends, for example, often depend on businesses introducing ideas; consumers then decide which of those ideas will become most popular.

> **Effective demand** is the combination of desire for a product or service with the ability and readiness to pay.
>
> **Consumer sovereignty** suggests that consumers control resource use by deciding what to buy.

Invisible hand

Adam Smith, observing how the market system works to allocate resources, described it as the 'invisible hand'. Increasing demand creates an incentive for businesses to produce more and meet that demand. If the resources needed to do this become scarce, costs rise and higher prices will make consumers buy less, and vice versa.

> **Show your understanding**
>
> Explain how the example of XDS above illustrates the idea of consumer sovereignty and the working of the invisible hand.
>
> Towards the end of 2014, several oil-producing countries were increasing their output of oil. The price fell. Explain why. Some people thought the price might rise again quite soon. Why might they have thought this?

Determinants of demand

Think of a particular cinema. On any evening, there will be effective demand from a number of people arriving to see films. The level of demand will depend on many different things.

Personal preferences

- How attractive do people find a cinema trip and the specific films on show? This is a question of **tastes**. The personal preferences which determine our tastes are partly shaped by experience, cultural background and even by mood and the seasons.

- **Advertising** and **branding** are attempts by businesses to influence demand by changing consumer tastes. Some advertising is simply giving information, but it may aim to persuade. Strong brands have an advantage over unknown alternatives.

Substitutes

- How attractive are alternative options such as the evening's television programmes? This is an example of the availability of **substitutes**. (The decline of the 'flying pigeon' has a lot to do with this).

- When two things are used together we call them **complementary goods**. Many people see popcorn and soft drinks as complementary to cinema visits. Transport to get to the cinema is also a complementary good.

- How many people can afford to go to the cinema? This depends on the level and distribution of **income**.

- How many people live within range of a cinema? This is a question of **population**.

- What is the **price** of tickets?

All seven of the variables identified above will influence the demand for cinema tickets. Each of them could be studied and analysed in more depth. For example, it is not just the existence of substitutes that is significant. One brand of trainers is a substitute for another just as cinemas are substitutes for each other. Whilst similar brands might be close substitutes, design and price of trainers varies so much that many consumers reject much of what is available and only consider a narrow range of possibilities. How close a substitute tenpin bowling or clubbing would be for a cinema trip depends on tastes. The price of each substitute makes a difference too.

The age structure of the population probably matters at least as much as its overall size. In a town with a very high proportion of retired people, demand for evening cinema trips might be relatively low but there could be a market for daytime films aimed at pensioners. If income distribution is very uneven, and young adults (who use cinemas more) tend to be poor, that will reduce demand for the cinema.

Demand

Figure 8.1: Determinants of demand

Tastes involve consumer preferences for specific products. These are likely to change over time and be influenced by factors such as fashion.

Advertising and **branding** are ways in which businesses try to influence demand for their products. They may succeed in changing tastes.

Substitutes are the alternatives to a product. Sometimes there are close substitutes (e.g. alternative brands of petrol), sometimes not.

Complementary goods tend to be used together or 'complement' each other. There are many examples such as theatre seats and programmes or mobile phones and music downloads.

Income is the flow of money received by an individual or household over time. Incomes are often a reward for economic activity.

Population: a group of people fitting a particular description, from the national population (total inhabitants) to the population in a target market (e.g. horse riders in and around a town).

Price is the money amount paid by the buyer to the seller in a transaction. This is usually set by market forces but can sometimes be regulated by governments.

Opportunity cost

Despite the possible complications from other influences on demand, the central element in demand theory is the relationship between price and quantity bought. Price plays a key role in deciding what people choose to buy. The higher the price we pay for something, the greater the opportunity cost will be. At a lower price, with a lower opportunity cost, a product should become more attractive and quantity demanded should increase. Just think of how much busier shops are during the sales and on 'Black Friday'. There is normally an inverse relationship between price and quantity demanded.

Figure 8.2: Inverse relationship

When P ↑	Q ↓
When P ↓	Q ↑

Analysing markets

When we need to analyse markets we use **demand schedules** and **demand curves** to show this fundamental relationship. A demand schedule lists prices and the relevant quantity sold; a demand curve is simply a diagram showing the link between the price charged and the level of demand. The convention is to show the price level on the vertical axis and quantity on the horizontal axis, with zero for both scales at the bottom left of the diagram. The curve should slope downwards from left to right, and even though we call it a curve we often draw it as a simple straight line.

Figure 8.3: Demand curve and schedule

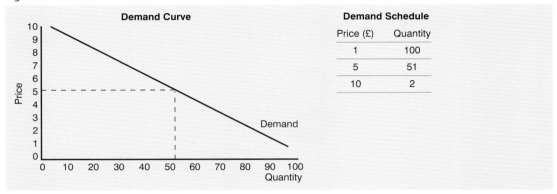

Demand Schedule	
Price (£)	Quantity
1	100
5	51
10	2

Movements along the demand curve

Price and quantity

It is important to understand and remember that any demand curve shows the relationship between price and quantity sold. It assumes that none of the other influences on demand changes. The whole point of the demand curve is to show this relationship. A rise in price will cause a movement up and left along the existing demand curve (called a **contraction of demand**). A fall in price causes a movement down and right along it (called an **extension of demand**).

A shift in the demand curve

A change in any of the other relevant factors will cause a **shift to a new demand curve**. A change which increases demand (such as a sudden fashion for the product) will move the curve to the right. If demand falls (e.g. because incomes fall), the curve shifts left.

> ⚠ **WATCH OUT!**
>
> Muddled students get tangled up between a movement along a demand curve (when price changes) and a shift to a new demand curve (when any other determinant changes). Stay clear on this.

Figure 8.4: Changes in demand

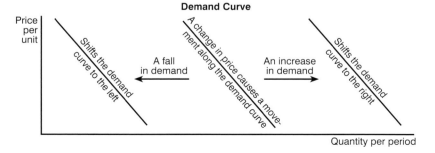

> **Demand schedule:** a table showing the quantities demanded at different price levels.
>
> **Demand curve:** a graphical representation of the relationship between quantity demanded and price, for a product in a market.
>
> **Contraction of demand:** move up and left on a demand curve when price rises.
>
> **Extension of demand:** move down and right on a demand curve when price falls.
>
> **A shift in the demand curve** occurs when quantity demanded changes for reasons other than price – e.g. a change in incomes or tastes and fashions.

Demand curves

Try this

1. Starting from the mental image of a cinema near you, make a rough estimate of how many customers would buy tickets this evening at £3, £5, £10 and £20 each.

2. Convert this information into a demand curve.

3. If the current price is £5, show the quantity of tickets sold at that price.

4. Draw diagrams to illustrate what happens (a) if the price rises to £7, (b) or if bad weather closes down local public transport and makes roads dangerous, (c) or if full time students in the area have all just received payment of a new type of maintenance grant.

Exam style question

Watching the trends

2013 US home entertainment revenue, by type

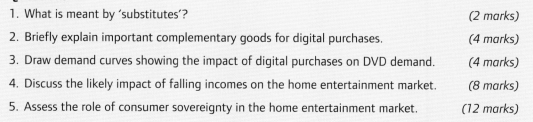

Type	2013 sales (billions)
Digital purchases	$1.19
Subscription streaming	$3.16
Video-on-demand rental	$2.11
Kiosk rental	$1.92
DVD/Blu-ray sales	$7.78
Rental from stores	$1.04
Disc subscription rental	$1.02

Source: DEG: The Digital Entertainment Group

Sales of DVD and Blu-ray discs are still the main source of revenue in the valuable U.S. home entertainment market, but sales fell by 8% in 2013. Rental of discs fell sharply as well. Digital substitutes for discs are the growth area of the market. Total market revenue is well below the 2004 peak of $22 billion.

Questions

1. What is meant by 'substitutes'? *(2 marks)*

2. Briefly explain important complementary goods for digital purchases. *(4 marks)*

3. Draw demand curves showing the impact of digital purchases on DVD demand. *(4 marks)*

4. Discuss the likely impact of falling incomes on the home entertainment market. *(8 marks)*

5. Assess the role of consumer sovereignty in the home entertainment market. *(12 marks)*

Chapter 9

Supply

Milk production

Higher milk prices during 2013 stimulated production in the UK and globally. In the first half of 2014, EU milk production was up 5%, New Zealand up 8.4%, USA up 1.4% and UK production for January to November 2014 was 9% up on 2013. With continued good weather and plentiful forage supplies, there is no sign on the horizon of milk supply falling in the short term.

Figure 9.1 clearly shows the consecutive months of high domestic milk production over the past year which have led to an abundance of supply. High domestic production, combined with the ban on dairy imports to Russia and falling returns from global markets, have resulted in a fall in milk prices. UK farmers operate in a global dairy market. Their exports account for a small percentage of milk produced, but have a major impact on price. Most UK milk processors have reduced their payments to farmers for raw liquid milk. Further price falls have been publicly announced by several large processors for the coming months.

Figure 9.1: UK milk production

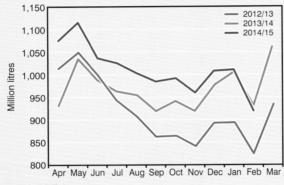

Source: AHDB/Dairyco

Discussion points

1. Why was the supply of milk higher in 2014 than earlier?

2. What are the consequences of UK farmers operating in a global market?

3. How might farmers react to falling milk prices?

A small business

Market forces

The case study above looked at a global market. In contrast, this next section is about an individual entrepreneur. In both cases market forces impact on the quantity of a product supplied in the market place. Producers have mixed objectives, as seen in Chapter 2. Whatever their market, the ability to earn profits and income has an influence on the choices made by almost all suppliers. Potential profits provide an incentive to supply.

Collins has his own small fishing business in Mombasa, Kenya. His main catch, for years, has been prawns. He knows where to find them along the coast, in waters that are too shallow for large, commercial fishing boats. His custom was to fish in the morning, and then to visit a series of regular customers in the afternoon. Many of them bought prawns at 60 shillings (Ksh) for a small bag. He could sell any surplus catch at the fish market, but generally for a lower price.

Changes across the world had an impact on Collins when prawn farming (in large ponds) became popular on other continents. Cheaper farmed prawns took over markets around the world. This left places like Mombasa with a local surplus as the larger commercial fishing businesses, which had previously sent their prawns to distant cities, lost those markets and sold locally instead.

**Market
signals**

The local price fell and Collins found his customers wanting two bags of prawns for 60Ksh before they would buy. Selling at this price reduced his income, even if he stayed out fishing for longer. He experimented with other catches and found that his customers enjoyed parrot fish, a tasty white fish found in his area. The amount of his catch was slightly more variable with parrot fish, but on a typical day he could catch enough to earn more than prawns now raised, selling them to his regular customers at 100Ksh each.

Collins began to watch the market prices and adjust what he caught and charged. He could catch prawns, parrot fish, or some of each. If the prices for both were high, he could stay out longer to catch more and earn more. When both prices were low he would catch just enough to pay for his family's necessities. A high price for either prawns or parrot fish gave him an incentive to specialise in whichever catch could earn him more.

Collins settled to a new pattern where his fishing and typical daily catches were influenced by prices. He still found catching prawns a little easier:

A supply schedule

Price of prawns (per bag)	Typical catch (bags)		Price of parrot fish (each)	Typical catch
25 Ksh.	20		25 Ksh.	0
50	50		50	40
75	80		75	60
100	110		100	80
125	120		125	90

**Supply
curves**

Figures such as these can be graphed and form the basis of a **supply curve**. When plotting supply and demand, we always measure quantity on the horizontal axis and price on the vertical axis. When we look at markets, we generally combine the quantities supplied by all the producers.

Figure 9.2: Supply of prawns

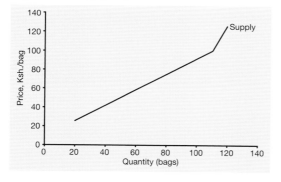

Figure 9.3: Supply of parrot fish

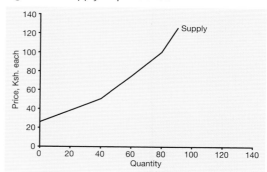

Supply curves

**Incentives
to supply**

Supply curves normally slope upwards from left to right, showing that less will be supplied at a low price and more at a high price. North Sea Oil producers drill in deep waters and have relatively high costs, but these were more than covered when the oil prices were around $110 per barrel in mid-2014. In the winter of 2014-15, prices fell to below $50 per barrel. British Petroleum (BP) and other producers reacted by reducing

North Sea production. They supplied less at a lower price. Oil prices are eventually likely to rise again. When this happens, North Sea producers will probably respond by once again increasing their output.

> **Try this**
> In February 2014 North Sea Oil sold at $100 per barrel and production was 850,000 barrels. A year later, at a price of $50 per barrel, some high cost oilfields were mothballed and production fell to 650,000 barrels (all data rounded). Assume that there was no other change in conditions of supply, and that output at $75 per barrel would be 750,000 barrels. Turn this information into a supply curve.

A higher price attracts producers to supply more. Even if their costs increase when producing more, a higher price increases revenue from sales. If the revenue increase is greater than the cost increase, profits will rise. This is the incentive which attracts extra supply. The fashion for selfie photos created a market for extra kit. The first selfie sticks (in Asia) sold well and prices rose. This led the makers to increase output and new firms to enter the market. More was supplied at a high price.

The positive relationship between price and quantity supplied is the opposite of demand (where the relationship is negative). Both supply and demand curves focus just on the influence of price on quantity, ignoring or freezing other possible influences. Figure 9.4 shows the effects of a change in price on the quantity supplied.

Figure 9.4: The effect of price changes on supply

When P ↑	Q ↑
When P ↓	Q ↓

> A **supply curve** is a graphical representation of the relationship between quantity supplied and price, for all suppliers in the market.

The long run

A supply curve refers to a specific market and a limited period of time. In the longer term more changes become possible. For example, the profitability of selfie sticks in Asia attracted new producers. After the time it took them to organise machinery and production, market supply increased – shifting the supply curve as shown in Figure 9.5. This longer term shift is likely to lead to a lower price and reduced profitability. Eventually, price and output are likely to settle at a steadier level.

The distinction here is that some changes to output can be made cheaply and quickly, such as buying more materials and asking workers to put in longer hours. We refer to the time period involved here as the **short run**. Adding to machinery and constructing buildings are examples of **long run** changes. The time periods involved are not precise and vary between industries. For example, building new nuclear power plant takes far longer than leasing and equipping a new tattoo parlour.

> In supply theory, the **short run** is the time period in which the quantity of at least one component in production cannot be changed.
>
> The **long run** is the time period in which the quantities of all factors of production can be changed.

In the short run, a price change causes a move along the supply curve. In the long run a move to a new supply curve is possible.

Short and long run changes in supply

Figure 9.5: Long run increase in supply

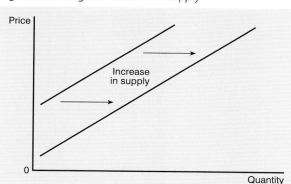

Other determinants of supply

- **Costs of production** have a major influence on supply. The biggest cost for Collins is his own time. A large milk producer will have financial costs, for the labour employed and for animal feed (more in winter), for example. If costs go up and nothing else changes, supplying the market becomes less profitable. Producers are likely to want a higher price to supply any quantity, so the supply curve is likely to move up and left.

- Producers are dependent on the **state of technology**. Collins has only basic equipment with a small boat and a net. Both larger fishing operations and milk producers take advantage of new technologies. For example, large 'milking parlours' are now highly automated and require less labour per litre or tanker of milk. Although the latest technology is often expensive, its success normally depends on reducing costs per unit. So a successful new technology will shift the supply curve to the right. This is an important component of economic growth.

- Government intervention can alter the balance of revenue and costs by adding **indirect taxes or subsidies**. The intention can be to reduce sales, to raise tax revenue, or both. The effect of an indirect tax on a product will be to increase the price to the customer. Many businesses feel the impact of taxes on fuel, for example. Farmers have benefitted from subsidies offsetting some costs.

- Supply to any market will be changed by the **entry and exit of firms**. A profitable market attracts more producers (entry). The success of early tablet computers a few years ago drew many producers into the industry, with sales growing to over 200 million units in 2013. If a product becomes unprofitable, firms will leave the industry and supply will decrease (exit).

Figure 9.6: Determinants of supply

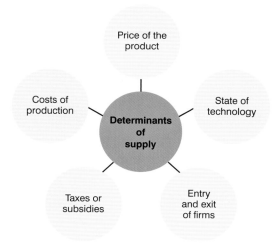

The passage on milk supply mentioned good weather and plentiful forage (grass and similar cattle food). (See case study on page 42). For the first two months of 2014, much of Somerset was flooded. Even if farmers could feed and milk their cows, the tankers that transport milk could not reach farms in flooded areas. This is an example of an external shock disrupting production. Weather events cause some shocks. Another cause is earthquakes and tsunamis. The dispute that closed the Russian market to milk producers (and others) shows that human activity can also bring unexpected impacts (shocks). (See page 42.)

Changing costs

When, as one example, technological change reduces costs and leads to an increase in supply, the supply curve shifts outwards to the right, as shown in Figure 9.5. A decrease in supply causes a shift left and inwards.

Figure 9.7: Increases and decreases in supply

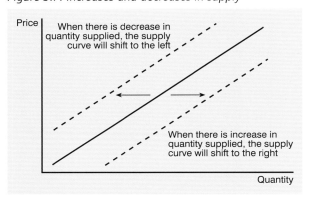

> ⚠ **WATCH OUT!**
>
> Shifting a supply curve up and left looks intuitively like an increase, but is not. This is a decrease as less will now be supplied at any price. Check this and try to learn it. Many students struggle on this point.

The labour market

Market forces

Markets for factors of production and for materials are subject to the same market forces as consumer goods. Most of us are involved in the labour market at some times. Looking at decisions on what to do to earn by working gives useful insights on supply. The cost of working is less centred on a money cost and more on the opportunity cost, such as leisure time given up.

When we work we supply our labour. Like most suppliers, we would generally like a higher price for what we supply rather than a lower one. If we supply unskilled labour our wage, the price for our work, is likely to be low. The supply of unskilled labour is plentiful so buyers (employers) can pay relatively little. Some people are so determined to work that they will supply their labour even at a very low price (where the law allows that). Longer hours mean giving more time up, often compensated for by higher overtime payments.

> **Think**
> Salaried professionals are rarely paid for overtime. What reasons might there be for this?

Earnings are higher in sectors of the labour market differentiated by training, skills and qualifications, experience and talent. The supply of such labour is more limited and in some cases very limited. A top plastic surgeon, for example, needs all of the listed attributes and the supply is very restricted. The supply of labour for work that is less pleasant (e.g. night shifts) or more dangerous (e.g. divers) will also be limited.

As with products, there is likely to be a bigger supply of any type of labour at a high price than at a low price. The higher reward should attract more supply, though perhaps after a time lag if training or qualifications are required. A supply curve for labour should also slope upwards from left to right.

Entry to specialist sections of the labour market often depends on education and training. This can be expensive but is often subsidised or provided by government. It is in the interests of society as well as the individuals for workers to become more skilled, more productive and higher paid. Work is not just a financial transaction; some of us are lucky enough to get satisfaction from what we do or contribute to society; we even sometimes enjoy our work. Like entrepreneurs, we have mixed objectives but nearly all find the income from work useful.

Exam style question

Cocoa supply

Around 3.5 million tonnes of cocoa are supplied each year. Around two thirds of this is produced in Africa, the remainder in the Americas and Asia. Rising incomes in emerging markets like India and China, and some economic recovery in rich developed countries, have led to industry forecasts of a 30% growth in demand to more than 4.5 million tonnes by 2020. This should be good news for farmers. But the industry may simply be unable to provide sufficient supply to meet the demand.

Even as cocoa prices rise, farmers have not been capturing their fair share. African growers are likely to receive just 3.5% to 6.4% of the final price of a chocolate bar, depending on the percentage of cocoa content – compared with 16% in the late 1980s. By contrast, the manufacturers' share has increased from 56% to 70% and the retailers' from 12% to 17% over the same period.

Low prices paid to farmers result in low productivity in farming communities. Farmers use out-dated farming methods and lack funds to invest in fertilisers or in replacing ageing trees past their peak productivity. As prices of food and other costs rise, failure to earn enough from their crop means that many cocoa farmers are exiting the industry.

Many of their children see no future in cocoa so switch to more profitable rubber production or head for the cities in the hope of finding a better income. As a result, the average age of cocoa farmers in West Africa is now 51, leading to concerns about the long-term sustainability of supply: no cocoa farmers = no chocolate bars. Chocolate makers such as Mars have warned of a 1m tonne supply deficit in 2020 if production is not increased.

Questions

1. What is meant by sustainability? (2 marks)

2. Illustrate and briefly explain the effect on the cocoa supply curve of farmers exiting the industry. (4 marks)

3. Explain how growing demand could normally attract increasing supply. (4 marks)

4. Discuss the opportunity cost of cocoa farming in West Africa. (8 marks)

5. Assess the relevance of the main determinants of supply to the possible shortage in 2020. (12 marks)

Chapter 10

How are prices fixed?

Holiday prices

I have kept my eye on a certain holiday on a major travel agent's website. I've checked it daily and the price drops and increases dramatically every single day! I am talking hundreds of pounds difference.

from Sheffield forum website

I have held off booking our holiday in February for ages, kept an eye on the prices and hedged my bets. Last week the prices went up to £590 from £579. When I went to book it online it said 'hurry one room left'. So I booked at £590. They then went up to £640. Just looked now and it is £470, how can they do that? Surely if prices are going up it's for a reason, the travel agent said it was because the plane was getting full! How can they just drop it by £120pp? That's £240 we could have saved.

from mumsnet.com

Prices shown on this website are believed correct at the time of publication. Prices found in our brochure may differ from those displayed on the website, and offers advertised on this website may not be available in the brochure. We reserve the right to change prices from time to time. Accordingly, it is possible that when you book your holiday the actual price may have gone up or down from the advertised price. If the price of your holiday has changed, the correct price will be confirmed before you book. We reserve the right to correct errors at any time prior to the price being confirmed at the time of booking.

from Monarch.co.uk

Discussion points

1. How is it possible for holiday prices to change frequently?
2. Why might holiday prices go up?
3. Why might holiday prices go down?

Equilibrium

A profitable price attracts producers to supply to a market. A rise in price is likely to attract more suppliers and more output.

- Supply curves show us that the quantity supplied tends to increase as the price level increases. The prospect of profit, a powerful incentive, attracts suppliers.

- Lower prices tend to attract more buyers to a product, as the opportunity cost of the product falls. Demand curves show us that more will normally be bought at a lower price than a higher price.

Competitive markets

It is the combination of demand and supply, interacting in a competitive market, which sets the market price. When demand and supply curves intersect, we have a market. The point at which the curves cross shows the equilibrium quantity for sale and purchase, and also shows the equilibrium price. Figure 10.1 shows an equilibrium price of £50 and quantity of 400.

Even though demand and supply curves slope in opposite directions, they are not guaranteed to cross. The demand for tennis racquets made of solid platinum is too low to match a supplier's costs at any quantity. In this case, the entire demand curve would be below the supply curve and there would be no functioning market.

Figure 10.1: Equilibrium price and quantity

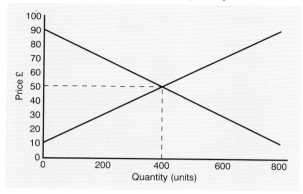

Note: sales revenue will be equilibrium price times quantity, £50 x 400 = £20,000 here.

> ⚠ **WATCH OUT!**
>
> You should ALWAYS label the axes and curves on a diagram. Failure to do this is penalised by examiners.

Excess supply and excess demand

 Market clearing

At any price above the equilibrium level, quantity supplied exceeds quantity demanded: there is **excess supply**. Sellers have a surplus which could only be sold by reducing price. A 'sale' would be one way of selling surplus stock. At a price below equilibrium, there is **excess demand** as consumers want more than firms will supply. Firms could easily sell out, but without getting the best possible price. Only at the equilibrium price will there be **market clearing**: the amount that sellers wish to supply just balances the amount that buyers demand. This is shown on Figure 10.2. In a competitive market, excess supply and excess demand will usually not last for long. Market forces will lead to a change in price.

Figure 10.2: Excess supply, excess demand and market clearing.

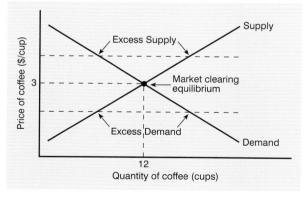

Disequilibrium

Excess supply occurs when the quantity supplied is greater than the quantity demanded. This disequilibrium would usually be caused by setting a price that is too high to attract enough customers to buy the quantity that suppliers are offering.

Excess demand occurs when the quantity demanded outstrips the quantity supplied. There is a shortage of the product. Raising the price will cause the customers to buy less and so restore equilibrium.

Equilibrium price is the price at which quantity supplied and quantity demanded are equal in a market, leaving neither excess supply nor excess demand.

Market clearing: obtaining a balance between quantity supplied and quantity demanded, normally by arriving at the equilibrium price.

Show your understanding

Describe one real world example of excess supply and one of excess demand. If you are having trouble with this, imagine a likely situation and describe that.

When might disequilibrium in a market last for some while?

Shifting the equilibrium

Shifts in supply

A change to any of the non-price determinants of supply or demand will shift one of the curves and so cause a shift to a new equilibrium price and quantity. The two market diagrams in Figure 10.3 show that an increase in supply should lead to a fall in price but a rise in quantity, whilst a fall in supply should bring a rise in price but a fall in quantity. For example, a fall in component costs could cause an increase in supply of computer tablets, whereas a rise in wages (a major cost) could cause a fall in supply.

Figure 10.3: Changes in supply

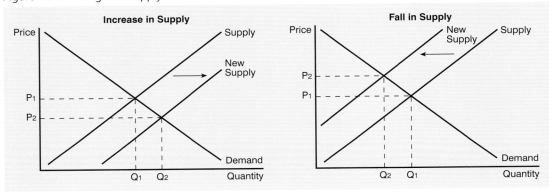

A rise in demand, say as tattoos become more popular, should lead to a rise in both price and quantity. By contrast, a fall in demand should result in both price and quantity falling. This has happened to foods linked with health scares, for example.

Shifts in demand

Figure 10.4: Changes in demand

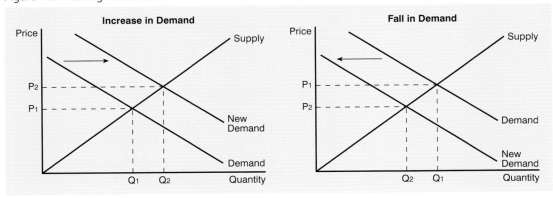

Note: Little arrows on diagrams (as above) are a good way of showing understanding of changes. Straight lines or curves are both generally acceptable. Straight lines are simpler to draw.

Try this

Just learning this theory is less useful than being able to use it.

Draw an initial supply and demand diagram representing the market for honey, and use it to show the effects of disease reducing bee numbers and honey supply. On a second diagram show the effects of a report that honey is healthier than other sweeteners, increasing demand. Show the new equilibrium in each case. Both changes should mean price goes up. What happens to quantity is less certain.

The profit signalling mechanism

Incentives

When the equilibrium price changes because demand has changed, this can trigger the **profit signalling mechanism**. A price increase, when demand rises, is likely to increase profits and this can both attract new producers and encourage existing firms to increase output. In the short run this brings a move along the supply curve. In the long run new entrants will shift the supply curve. Profits provide the incentive to enter markets; losses lead firms to close down or reduce production.

Example

When the UK economy was shrinking or growing very slowly, there was a fall in demand for do-it-yourself products to maintain and improve homes. D-I-Y stores became less profitable. Some closed and their premises were transferred to more profitable alternative uses. This fall in demand is shown as the shift from D to D_1 in Figure 10.5. Initially, a short-term shift down and left on supply curve S would mean falls in quantity sold, price and profits. In time, businesses might react to this by reducing supply (e.g. by closing some stores); this would cause a shift from S to S_1. Prices might recover, but quantity would fall further.

Figure 10.5: The market for D-I-Y materials

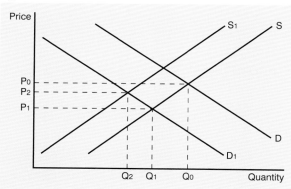

Think

Have any D-I-Y stores closed in your area?

If so, what has happened to their buildings?

Have any new ones opened? If so, why?

Profit

UK demand for private medical services has grown in the last two decades. Healthy demand allows private clinics to make a profit, to build new premises and to offer attractive salaries to recruit staff. Profits have drawn more resources into this sector. An increase in demand has increased profits and this acted as a signal for firms to increase supply.

> The **profit signalling mechanism** refers to the way that potential profits will attract entrepreneurs to a growing market; losses will lead businesses to consider leaving a market. This process shifts resource use towards the products that are most in demand.

Prices in a dynamic economy

Price determination

Whenever a price changes, there has been a change in supply conditions, in demand, or in both. Where prices stay unchanged over a long period of time, this is often the result of suppliers choosing stability, absorbing any cost changes and living with reduced profit.

Some prices can be 'sticky' and only change infrequently; other prices are very volatile. For example, the stock exchange can see prices changing for a particular share many times in a day; like other price changes this reflects a change in supply or demand. With so many variables in the business environment, price fluctuations are entirely normal.

> **Think**
> Can you identify two products with 'sticky' prices and two markets where prices change frequently?

Technology allows suppliers such as holiday companies and supermarkets to adjust prices frequently in response to market conditions. If, for example, a holiday business has arranged flights to a destination and reserved hotel rooms, a flow of holiday bookings showing healthy demand might encourage the business to raise prices. As each departure date draws near, there is a case for reducing prices if that will help to fill remaining spare capacity.

Using the model

Our price determination model simplifies reality, making unrealistic assumptions, and we normally look at only one variable at a time. We rely on a '**ceteris paribus**' assumption which means that everything stays unchanged except the one thing we focus on. So, for example, when we look at supply in a market we assume that demand conditions stay fixed. It is quite possible, though, that both supply and demand conditions change at the same time. Although firms have some information about current demand, they can't always be confident about the shape of the demand curve and whether it is changing.

We assume that supplying businesses are motivated simply by profit (see Chapter 2) and that competition forces them to react to changing conditions in predictable ways. Global energy prices fell from the autumn of 2014, due partly to increased supply of oil and gas from fracking in the USA. The crude oil price fell from above $100 per barrel to below $50. In early November 2014, Treasury minister Danny Alexander wrote to major petrol retailers and distributors urging them to cut retail prices when wholesale prices fall. He wrote: *"the public have a right to expect pump prices to fall like a stone, not like a feather."*

Think

Why might businesses be reluctant to cut prices when their costs fall?

Competition

Pump prices did fall early in 2015 and attention switched to the major gas and electricity suppliers, whose prices were also slow to fall (though much electricity generation is powered by gas and oil). In this situation, competition does not seem strong enough to bring a rapid shift in supply curves when costs fell. Real world complexities include the fact that wholesale energy prices are often fixed for some time by 'future' contracts, but also that major energy suppliers often buy from producers owned by the same organisation. This reduces the impact of competition, which would normally ensure a change in price.

Although it is simplified, our model of price determination does capture some important basic factors and provides a foundation on which much of economics is built.

> The simplifying **ceteris paribus** assumption freezes all variables other than the one being studied, avoiding complications and allowing us to examine individual changes. Ceteris paribus is Latin for 'other things being equal'.

Exam style question

Price of bread to rise by 25p a loaf

In 2013, a report by retail consultancy Conlumino suggested that food prices would soar by nearly 20% over the next five years, due to a worsening shortage of food on a global scale. The staggering hike would see an average family's household food bill shoot up by £850 a year while the nation's annual food bill would rise by £19.6 billion. The inflation-busting increase would cause the price of a loaf of sliced bread to rise by 25p while a pint of milk would cost nine pence more. This suggests that the growing global demand for meat and grain as well as the erratic weather is to blame. "Out of all sectors on the high street, food will see the highest inflation between now and 2018."

Source: Adapted from the *Daily Mail*

Table 10.1: Bread prices (800g white sliced loaf)

Year	Price p (rounded)
1980	30
1985	40
1990	50
1995	50
2000	55
2005	65
2010	120
2015	110

Source: ONS

Questions

1. What is meant by global demand? *(2 marks)*
2. Explain growing global demand for bread. *(4 marks)*
3. Illustrate and explain the effect of erratic weather on supply. *(4 marks)*
4. Discuss the likely impact of cost inflation on the price of bread. *(8 marks)*
5. Assess **two** possible reasons why bread prices have fallen since 2010 *(12 marks)*

Chapter 11

How does the price mechanism work?

Tablet computers

A tablet computer has a touch-screen, circuitry and a battery in a single unit and often additional features such as cameras and a microphone. Prototypes were developed over many years in the 20th century. Rapid sales growth began with the introduction of the Apple iPad in 2010. The Android operating system had over 60% of sales in 2013-14, with iOS, Windows and open source systems taking smaller shares of the market. Rapid growth of tablet sales continued in 2014, but new products such as phablets (small tablets with phones) are gaining in popularity.

Table 11.1: Global tablet sales

Year	2010	2011	2012	2013	2014
Sales (m)	17.6	60.0	116.3	195.4	230 (est)
% growth	–	240.9	93.8	68.0	12.2

Source: Wikipedia

Discussion points

1. What resources are required for tablet production and sales?

2. What explains the rapid growth of tablet sales?

3. How relevant is creative destruction to products such as tablets?

Consumer sovereignty

Earlier in this book we saw that choices must be made to decide how scarce resources will be used. We've also seen that consumer sovereignty plays an important part in markets. The rapid growth of tablet sales depended on new technologies that reduced production costs and then prices, but that would have had little effect if tablets had not appealed to consumers.

In 2011, tablet prices were way above 2015 prices but consumers were willing to buy them. It paid businesses to use resources to develop the product because it would be profitable. In this way prices act as **market signals**, guiding businesses on how to use the resources available.

Prices also act as a **rationing** device. You might like the idea of driving the LaFerrari, introduced in 2014 and described as "the king of all exotic sports cars." However, the price of close to £1million is an effective obstacle to most of us. As an alternative, you could use a taxi or perhaps even public transport if the taxi fare puts you off. An auction is a classic rationing device; only the highest bidder gets the use of each auctioned 'lot'.

Incentives

Your **incentive** not to go by taxi could be that the opportunity cost is too great; you value some other use of your income more. Sales give a greater incentive to buy because we expect better value for money. Ferrari's incentive for producing the LaFerrari is associated with confidence that there will be buyers at a profitable price. Tablet producers are motivated by that same incentive, with rising demand attracting suppliers. Market prices give a variety of prompts for action or inaction.

Price mechanism functions:

Signalling: prices give signals to producers and consumers.

Rationing: only those willing and able to pay the price get the products or resources.

Incentives: profitability motivates firms; value for money motivates consumers.

Strengths of the price mechanism

The price mechanism has two advantages:

- It works automatically, following decisions taken by a multitude of economic agents.
- It can direct resources to the best possible use.

Resource allocation

Each individual thinks about their own welfare in making decisions. We feed these decisions into the price mechanism by making spending choices that fuel the process of resource allocation. Consumers ultimately have control and should logically choose the resource uses which give them the greatest welfare or satisfaction.

Economic models

The logical steps in this analysis are set out in Figure 11.1, which illustrates the **economic model** of the price mechanism. Economic models are simplified structures that help us to analyse the way the economy works and to draw conclusions about how specific events change outcomes. In this case, the model explains how the **allocation of resources** changes in response to changing consumer preferences.

Figure 11.1: Resource allocation

Resource owners want maximum income so sell to the highest bidder

|

Firms bid for resources up to their value in revenue they can earn

|

Revenue firms can earn depends on what consumers will pay for output

|

What consumers will pay depends on welfare/benefit of consumption to them

|

Consumers will pay most for products offering the greatest welfare

|

Firms offering most welfare bid most so buy and use scarce resources

---

Economic models use simplified assumptions to describe economic relationships. These allow us to isolate individual changes and analyse their consequences, avoiding the complications that occur when several things are changing at once. Their success depends on how realistic the assumptions are. Supply and demand theory gives us a useful model for analysing the effects of any change that will influence price or quantity sold.

The **allocation of resources** reflects the way in which economic agents take decisions about what to buy, what to produce and how best to use the available land, labour and capital.

The **price mechanism** is an economic model that helps to explain the allocation of resources between different possible uses. It shows how the invisible hand guides resources towards production of what consumers will buy.

Economic models depend on reasonable assumptions but these are not always realistic. One assumption is that competition promotes cost efficiency and low prices; this works in some but not all markets. Another assumption is that consumers are 'rational', making logical choices. This too is true, sometimes.

Income distribution

Less obviously, the model of the price mechanism makes no reference to income distribution. Reports tell us that the wealthiest 1% own half of global wealth (Oxfam data) and receive 47% of income in the USA (OECD data). This means that many spending decisions which determine resource use are dominated by the very rich. Resources are used for LaFerrari whilst many people are homeless and/or hungry. Many people observe that poverty increased in the UK in the period 2010-15, whilst the incomes of top earners grew fast. The price mechanism sheds no light on this.

Consumer sovereignty

Creative destruction

Figure 11.1 states that what firms can earn depends on what consumers will pay for their output. This means that consumer demand ultimately decides how resources are used.

There is a long term trend in the UK towards cooking less at home and buying more take-away food and meals out. Town centres have seen many shops converted to take-away food from other uses. Reductions in sales of drinks in public houses (pubs) led to 31 closures per week in 2014 (*The Guardian*), with premises going to alternative uses. Other pubs have survived by developing food sales and extending eating areas, focusing on a growing market rather than a shrinking one.

Example
Demand for video tapes (and VHS players) has fallen away to nothing. Consumers now use DVDs or download. Unprofitable prices have led to businesses and resources moving away from video manufacture to other uses. Technological changes contribute to creative destruction such as this, but the key factor is consumer preference for the new product. In 1992 Nintendo introduced 'The Virtual Boy', a virtual reality headset intended to transform the future of gaming. It was attractively priced and used contemporary technology. Consumers didn't take to it and prices crashed; production quickly stopped. In this case, extensive marketing failed to modify consumer tastes.

Try this
Draw a demand and supply diagram to show the situation Nintendo hoped for with The Virtual Boy. Draw horizontal and vertical lines at the equilibrium price and quantity to show sales revenue (p x q). Now add another demand curve showing much lower demand, and then show the effect on revenue.

Mass markets

Homogeneous products

Some products are used by most people, so bought and sold in very large quantities. Quite often, these products are standardised or **homogeneous**, with little or no difference between what is offered by different suppliers. Milk and sliced white bread are good examples, so are many commodities and raw materials (e.g. copper or sugar). It is difficult for producers to **differentiate** their product to make them stand out from the competition.

Differentiated products

Large scale production allows firms to keep production costs low; competition in **mass markets** tends to be based on price. Milk is again a good example. In 2014, many supermarkets were selling milk for less than bottled water and less than the cost of production. Milk is also a 'known price item'; people tend to remember current prices.

> **Homogeneous** products are uniform, identical whatever their origin. All bananas look similar.
>
> **Differentiated** products are distinctive, with different design features or branding.
>
> In **mass markets**, products are supplied in significant quantities to all or most types of customers.

Growth, mergers and privatisation can all create large firms that build strong positions in some mass markets. Examples range from Coca Cola and British Gas to Google and Microsoft. Where there are several large firms and each has a significant market share, there is an oligopoly. This can change the nature of competition. Oligopolists watch each other's actions closely and respond. If one brings out a new product, others may follow suit or they increase their advertising spend to try to maintain market share. Competition may be quite fierce. The largest firms may have considerable market power.

Figure 11.2: Strong competition in mass markets

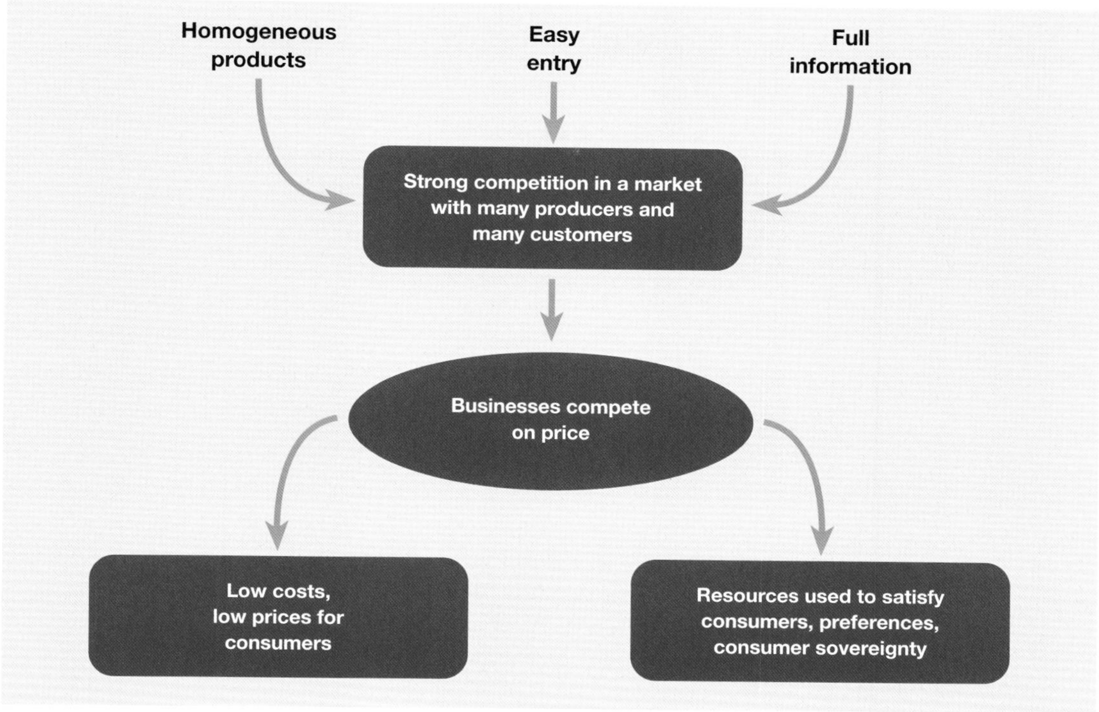

Competition

Table 11.2: Some UK oligopoly markets (2014)

Market	Oligopolists	Market Share %	Market Leader	Market Share %
Domestic energy	6	92	British Gas	33
Mobile networks	4*	80	EE	32
Groceries	4	73	Tesco	29

Source: Adapted from *The Guardian* and Kantar Worldwide.   *Note: A merger between two of these networks currently seems probable

Oligopoly is a market structure with a few large firms dominating the market. There are often smaller firms competing as well. Oligopolists are present in many mass markets.

Firms acquire **market power** when they can differentiate the product and control the amount produced and the price charged.

Niche markets

Niche markets are smaller and tend to work differently. They are specialised segments of a larger market, separated by particular needs or preferences. For example, organic foods offer a niche market, those customers most concerned for the environment and those who think organic offers better nutrition. There are mass markets in pet products for cats and dogs and a niche market for reptiles as pets.

Examples

American Marla Cilley spotted a niche website opportunity and makes money (as 'Flylady') by nagging her 550,000 e-mail subscribers to do things such as get up and get dressed for work, polish their sink, get their nails done, cook dinner and even to go to bed. Londoner Demi Owiseje grew her hobby of restoring specialist vintage furniture into 'Majeurs Chesterfield', a successful niche business.

Niche markets

Small firms in mass markets may be dwarfed by the large scale and market power of the biggest producers; they may make more profit in niche markets. They can start on a small scale, with a modest initial investment. If they can accurately meet the needs of their niche customers, they can build up a reputation and customer loyalty. Successful niche suppliers face less direct competition and can sometimes charge premium prices. They can acquire market power within their niche. Becoming a big fish in a small pond can be more profitable than being a relatively small fish in an ocean. Where highly specialised niches offer only tiny sales in one locality, online trading allows a business to cater for far away customers.

> **Example**
> The Charity Engine (based in Manchester) aims to tap into the spare computing power of the world's PCs for use on scientific projects. Users are incentivised to download its app in return for cash prizes and charities also share in the profits. "It's the world's cheapest, greenest and potentially most powerful computing platform, all from spare computing power that nobody was using anyway," says founder Mark McAndrew.

> **Niche market:** a small segment of a market with distinctive, specialised requirements. They may be associated with subcultures – groups of people with common interests.

Potential market growth

Markets and economies are not static. Some markets will be growing while others are shrinking. Some niche markets will become mass markets, others will eventually die out. Changing tastes are one factor here. The mass tourism market still offers sun, sea and sand holidays, now alongside a growing proportion of cultural holidays. There are niche markets for holidays spent volunteering for a range of activities, for development projects or archaeological digs, for example. How big these markets will grow is difficult to estimate.

Structural change

Changing technology is often involved in changes to markets. A hundred years ago, a few rich households had their own generator systems but most homes had no access to electricity. Markets for all electrical products were then niche markets, whereas fridges, washing machines, televisions and other electrical items are now very clearly mass market products. Vinyl music recordings were overtaken in the mass market by CDs and then downloads, but there is still a niche market for those who prefer vinyl records. Mobile telephone sales expanded into the mass market in the 1990s. We have reached the point where there are as many handsets as there are people on the planet, with some people using multiple phones and relatively few areas not yet reached. Fixed line telephone markets are shrinking.

This is the process of creative destruction identified by Joseph Schumpeter. The diagram below shows the sequence involved:

Figure 11.3: Technological and structural change

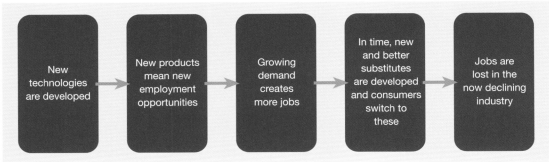

Business growth

- The Kraft Food Group started in 1903 with its founder's $65 capital, buying cheese from wholesalers and selling it on. It grew both internally by expanding existing business and externally by mergers and takeovers (including Cadbury in the UK). In 2013, before the group split itself into two parts, sales reached $18 billion per year. In 2015, Heinz took over the remaining Kraft operations to create a $100 billion business.

- Jack Cohen started in 1919 with a market stall in East London and grew the business (as Tesco) to sell 30% of groceries in the UK.

- Some internet based businesses grew faster. Page and Brin registered Google Inc. in 1997, having started work together a year earlier. By 2013, sales were $38 billion. Facebook is younger, starting as a niche business serving Harvard students in 2004, yet now with annual sales of over $100 billion. The potential for market growth can be almost beyond comprehension.

Exam style question

Changing resource use

One key feature of the UK industrial revolution from around 1750 was the growth of the canal network. A narrowboat could carry ten times the freight of a road cart, and at least as quickly. The total of navigable canals grew to around 4,000 miles. Railways were quicker and more efficient and brought creative destruction to canal freight in the 19th century. About half of the canal network was lost, some land went to urban development and many canals became unusable through neglect.

Slow erosion of the network continued until around 1970. Then a growing appreciation of the slow pace of canal life and the often attractive surroundings led to increasing leisure use. This coincided with reductions in the working week giving people more leisure time. Restoration projects have taken place in many parts of the country. More land has been used for marinas to act as boat parks. Pressures in the housing market have also brought growing use of narrowboats as homes, with alternatives expensive and difficult to find. In 2014, there were estimated to be 15,000 people living on canal narrowboats, the majority in London where the housing shortage is greatest.

Questions

1. What is meant by creative destruction? *(2 marks)*

2. Explain one way that recent technological changes might have made living on narrowboats more attractive than it was previously. *(4 marks)*

3. Briefly explain two new niche market opportunities from 21st century canal use. *(4 marks)*

4. Discuss likely recent changes in the narrowboat market. *(8 marks)*

5. Assess the case for further extending and improving the canal network. *(12 marks)*

Chapter 12

Understanding the consumer

Cut & Dried

Stephanie felt ready for changes in her working life. A trained and talented hairdresser, she had run a travelling service on a part-time basis for several years. This entailed working with clients in their homes at mutually convenient times, though finding times had grown harder as her reputation spread and more would-be customers contacted her. With her older child about to transfer to secondary school, arrangements for a return to full-time work would become easier.

A printing business near her home had closed. Most of the premises, and a new extension, were becoming flats. At the front of the building, facing a busy road, a shop unit was taking shape. With some additions to the planned plumbing and electrical work, it could make a good sized hairdressing salon. Working for someone else would be safer, but the idea of running her own salon, and doing things her own way, appealed to Stephanie. The building's owners were interested in her proposal. They wanted a decision within three weeks in order to add any changes to their building plans.

Discussion points

1. How important was it for Stephanie to do some research before making a decision about the shop?

2. What information would be valuable to her?

3. Give examples of relevant things that could be looked up and of things Stephanie would need to find out for herself.

Market research

Advance planning

Starting a business or launching a new product both involve significant up-front costs. These include:

- product development
- investment in equipment and premises
- spending on initial marketing.

Businesses try to ensure that these expenses carry the minimal possible risk. In order to do this they conduct **market research**. Gathering this information will allow them to be more confident that investing in the new idea will be profitable in the long term.

The table below shows how market research can reduce risk when developing a new business idea:

Market research

Purpose – allows the entrepreneur to:	Procedure
Quantify potential demand	Using the results of market research, entrepreneurs can forecast future sales. This allows them to estimate future revenue.
Understand how much customers are willing to pay	An entrepreneur can assess whether the price that people will pay covers costs of production.
Understand customer behaviour	Finding out exactly who the product appeals to (and why) helps a business to sell in the right places and promote products effectively. It may also identify demand for something currently unavailable; this creates an incentive to explore a possible new product.
Study competitors and unique selling points (USPs)	Checking that a business idea is able to survive the competition and ideally stand out from rivals.
Identify key features of the business environment	To study whether social, legal, economic, political and technological factors are favourable to the new business idea.

Types of market research

Secondary research

A lot of the questions that businesses have about their new idea may have already been answered by other organisations. Examining such data sources is known as **secondary** or **desk research**. This name comes from the fact that the information is 'second hand' to the business that is using it. Researchers can simply view it from their desks.

Primary research

When the business can't find answers to their questions from an existing source, they will carry out their own research, known as **primary** or **field research**. This name comes from the fact that the information is gathered 'in the field'. The researchers will be looking directly at the market and the information they collect is 'first hand' to the person doing it.

> **Market research** is the process of gathering data in order to understand current and future customer needs and the nature of the marketplace. This reduces the risks in developing a new business idea.
>
> **Primary market research** is obtained 'first hand' by the business that is interested in the results. It involves fieldwork and can be directly related to the needs of the individual business. This is also known as **field research**.
>
> **Secondary market research**, also known as desk research, uses data that has been gathered previously by another organisation. It is often freely available.

Different approaches to primary research

Market research can also be categorised in another way, according to the type of data collected. If the research produces numbers, such as quantities or percentages, it is **quantitative research**. This might generate estimates of future sales or preferred shopping habits and times, or the details of an ideal product.

Other situations might require **qualitative research**. One example is the psychology of the potential customers – their opinions or feelings about the product. This kind of data cannot be put into numbers.

But it can reveal a great deal about consumer perceptions, attitudes and behaviour.

Quantitative research

Qualitative research

> **Quantitative market research** – market research conducted where the results are numerical and can be analysed statistically.
>
> **Qualitative market research** – market research to examine opinions and feelings.

Both primary and secondary research can be quantitative or qualitative. Good market research will link qualitative and quantitative data to build a detailed picture of customers' preferences.

"Now give us your spontaneous response"

Ways of conducting primary market research

Surveys	Questionnaire/survey	Asking people a pre-planned set of open or closed questions to gather qualitative or quantitative data respectively.
		Questionnaires can use post or phone surveys, or personal interviews. Design should be clear, relevant, logical, sequenced and not intrusive. Closed questions give a choice of answers and provide quantitative data. Open-ended questions are wide-ranging and provide qualitative information.
		Comment: this could be very detailed, or could consist of asking a few friends or colleagues two or three simple questions about an idea.
Focus groups	Focus group	Organising a group discussion on a topic led by the researcher. The research is always qualitative and attempts to capture the perceptions, reactions and attitudes of the group. For example, a group might discuss a planned advertisement or change in branding or their attitude to competitors. Results could be used to refine the business idea or plan a new product that exploits the weaknesses of rivals. Running a focus group requires complex skills. Hiring specialists can be expensive. Many small businesses cannot afford this type of research.
Observation	Observation	Watching and studying the actions of consumers, suppliers and rivals. This can include:
		• counting the footfall (including the type of person) passing a retail site to assess the suitability of the location.
		• observing how customers move around a store to learn how to position products for better sales.
		• studying the products or prices of a competitor to spot a potential gap in the market.
		• gathering information on the shortfalls of other products or services, to spot a gap in the market.
		Comment: This can be quite quick and simple for an entrepreneur without specialist marketing skills. It is also generally free.

**Test
marketing**

| Test marketing | Launching a product in a small area and evaluating the response to it. This avoids the cost of a 'national' launch if results are poor. |
| | *Comment:* small scale test marketing could mean asking friends to try a new recipe or providing a free service in return for feedback. |

Ways of conducting secondary research

Market reports	Organisations such as Mintel and Key Note produce reports on trends in the market, which are sold to businesses.
Government data	National and local government provide data on population demographics. The age, gender and income distribution in an area are available.
Economic historic and forecast data	Trends in unemployment, growth, inflation and consumer spending can be useful.
Internet	Search engines offer data on competitors in the relevant market.
Trade publications	Many industries have specialist magazines reporting on market trends. For example, *The Grocer* reports on trends in the grocery market.

Which method is best?

**Primary vs.
secondary
research**

Primary and secondary research each have distinctive advantages and disadvantages. Many businesses find that a combination works best, with primary research following some secondary research that can contribute useful background information. Businesses need to balance three key issues: cost, time and ease of data collection.

	Primary research	**Secondary research**
Advantages	• Is up to date as it is conducted as required. • Can be tailored to the precise needs of the business. • Can produce data which rivals do not have access to.	• Is available immediately. • May be inexpensive or free. • Normally cheaper than primary research. • Provides information on market size and market share.
Disadvantages	• Can be expensive. • Can be time consuming to collect and interpret data. • Methods such as focus groups can require specialist skills.	• May be out of date. • Difficult to guarantee accuracy. • Can be expensive to purchase (e.g. market reports). • Rivals can access this data too.

Try this

Thinking back to Stephanie's business idea and the research you identified, was there a mix of primary and secondary research?

After reading these pages, have you identified more research that would be useful for her?

Market or product orientation?

Product development

Product orientated businesses seek to create and develop a technically impressive product and then try to sell it to the consumer. Since the 1980s this approach has become much less common, particularly for technologically innovative products. (However, Steve Jobs of Apple famously said "A lot of times, people don't know what they want until you show it to them.")

Market orientated businesses concentrate on consumer preferences. By focusing on the wants and needs of the customer, they are much more likely to produce a product or service that the customer wants and will buy. This creates a competitive advantage over rivals, which may not be so closely focused on the customer.

Figure 12.1: Market and product orientation

> **Show your understanding**
> Identify three products that you think are likely to be product orientated and three that are likely to be market orientated. Explain why you have chosen each of them.

Sampling

Sampling issues

Research which includes *all* potential customers is likely to be impossibly expensive. Market research often involves **sampling**, particularly where quantitative primary research is required. Sampling is quicker, easier and cheaper than trying to involve everyone. Surveys and questionnaires gather information from a sample of consumers. Larger samples give a more reliable reflection of views across the population. A business faces a trade-off between accuracy, (larger is better) and cost or time (smaller is better), when setting a sample size.

Potential bias

The people in the sample must be selected carefully, otherwise it may have a **bias** towards the views of one particular group. Shoppers leaving Marks & Spencers would give different opinions from shoppers leaving Primark, for example. A *convenience sample* is the name for questioning people who happen to be nearby. This is easy but results are unreliable.

> **Think**
> How are shoppers in Marks and Spencer likely to differ from Primark shoppers, by age and income? Think of another example of sampling which would probably give biased results.

Types of sample

- A **random sample** could be more representative by taking, say, every 100th name from the electoral register. This can be expensive: it might involve visiting people several times, and some might be reluctant to answer questions.

- An alternative is a **quota sample**. A researcher ensures that responses from different groups of individuals accurately reflect the distribution of those groups in the whole population. So there would be representative groups by age, gender, occupation and perhaps other factors too. Interviewing the required number of each group can get the percentage of each type of person in the sample.

- Another alternative is **stratified sampling**, i.e. selecting from a particular segment of the population. For example, a new mobile phone might be targeted at young adults so sampling could focus on the intended age range.

Sampling involves collecting data from a number of people to represent the target market or the population as a whole.

Bias occurs when information collected from a sample does not accurately reflect variations in the total population. This is likely if the sample is small or inappropriately selected.

A **random sample** is one in which everyone has an equal chance of being selected.

A **quota sample** involves dividing the target market into groups according to their consumer characteristics; a percentage of the sample will be allocated to each group.

Stratified samples are similar to quota samples but can select participants within the target groups on a random basis, to gain greater accuracy.

The limitations of market research

Research pitfalls

Careful market research can be very costly. It also involves fine judgements, especially in relation to qualitative research. So it does have its limitations. If sufficient care is not taken when planning the research, the findings may be inaccurate. Large businesses can bear the costs of market research quite easily; smaller businesses will be limited in what they can do because their sales revenue will not cover the cost of extensive primary research. In particular:

- Market research is particularly tricky in foreign markets. Businesses need well-trained local people to help them and this too is very costly.

- Some markets change very rapidly; they are so dynamic that it may be impossible for market research to keep up with current trends.

- Production decisions may be take by managers who are unfamiliar with their markets and have not fully understood the need for or the implications of market research.

⚠ **WATCH OUT!**

Market research is often much more sophisticated than just doing questionnaires. In fact, very little market research is done this way. Instead, a lot of research is done using observation and focus groups to get a deeper understanding of the customers and the market. Observing people can include some who wouldn't fill in a questionnaire, and what people do might prove more reliable than what they say.

Market segmentation

Coca-Cola is the leading global brand in carbonated soft drinks. Innocent Smoothies was a slightly quirky producer of fruit smoothies, seemingly focused on ethics and fun as much as profits. In 2009 Coca-Cola bought 18% of Innocent. One of Innocent's founders suggested that Coke's marketing and buying power would help them "make Innocent a global brand and take its ethical values to the world's consumers."

In 2013 Coca-Cola took full control with 90% of the shares. The original founders kept a small share but said "we're not going to be the guys that make the ultimate decisions any more." Coke will continue to use the Innocent brand and made a commitment to keep Innocent's ethical ideals.

Questions
1. What impact would the acquisition of Innocent have on Coca-Cola's market share?
2. What other benefits might Coca-Cola get from owning the company?

Targeting specific tastes

Personal tastes vary. They depend on individual preferences but they are also influenced by the kind of person you are. **Market segmentation** identifies different groups in society and studies their particular needs and wants.

Some products aim at a mass market – we all buy toothpaste. But even in that market, producers have identified a range of different needs. They produce differentiated products, e.g. toothpaste for sensitive teeth or with whitening qualities. A few products sell well in mass markets that run across all sections of society – e.g. milk and unleaded petrol. But many markets for consumer products have segments that require different versions of the product to meet group needs precisely.

Think
Does ownership of Innocent give Coca-Cola access to new market segments?

How valuable is the acquisition of a brand with a healthier and ethical image?

Products and segments

Products for segmented markets	Markets segmented by
Package holidays e.g. cheap beach holidays, safaris, exotic locations	Age, income, interests
TV stations, e.g. ITV1, BBC4, Sky 1	Age, education, hobbies
Housing – starter homes, flats, houses	Income, location, family size

Market segmentation means identifying different groups of consumers in a market where each group has distinctive preferences. Products and marketing strategies can be differentiated to suit individual segments.

Exam style question (Section C)

Evaluate the importance of market research to a start-up business such as Cut & Dried.

(20 marks)

Chapter 13

How do firms compete?

Citroën C4 Cactus

Advertised features of the Cactus include 'bold and original', an 'expressive light signature', 'Airbump' side protection, 'striking and modern' and 'exceptional fuel economy'.

Prices start at £12,990.

The Cactus looks very different from the LaFerrari mentioned in Chapter 11. Its market is not at all like commodity markets such as cocoa or wheat, with standardised products. Cars are aimed at specific market segments. Most carmakers have a range of models to suit different types of customer.

Discussion points

1. Identify the significance of 'bold and original' and of the stated price of the Cactus.

2. What does the information above suggest to you about the target market for the Cactus?

3. Do you expect large quantities of the Cactus to sell in the UK?

Market positioning

Where a market is segmented, there are likely to be two or more variables influencing which segment the product is aimed at. In the case of cars there are many variables such as price, size, visual appeal, fuel consumption and safety. Consumers in different market segments will prioritise different features. If a business can find and target a gap in the market – essentially a combination of features for a neglected segment – it will face relatively little competition. This is **market positioning**, designing a product to fit the preferences of a target market segment. Citroen hope that the Cactus will meet the needs of a particular group of consumers better than its rivals do.

Marketing can be used to **reposition** a business. Sometimes a product loses its attractions in its target market or a business wants to expand to a larger market segment. Lucozade did this; as a nutritional product helping recovery from illness, its market was small and shrinking. Repackaged and advertised differently, it sells well as an energy drink for fitness enthusiasts.

Market mapping

Plotting key product features on a diagram, then showing where brands fit in terms of these features, is called **market mapping** (see Figure 13.1 and the market map for cars, Figure 13.2). This helps to identify gaps and so decide on market positioning for new products. Software exists to include multiple variables, but two dimensional diagrams show a clearer picture. Variables that could be mapped include:

Feature	
High quality v. basic quality	Male v. female
Mass v. niche market	Old v. young
Modern v. traditional	Urban customers v. rural customers
Aesthetic v. functional	High income customers v. low income customers
Luxury v. value	Complex technology v. simple

Figure 13.1: Market mapping: The idea

+ High (Variable Two)

Product A	**Product B**
+ High (Variable One)	– Low (Variable One)
Product C	**Product D**

– Low (Variable Two)

A market map identifies two specific product features (one on each axis). It uses market research findings to show where each brand fits. This reveals where in the market the competition is stiffest and where there are market segments with few competing products.

Figure 13.2: The car market

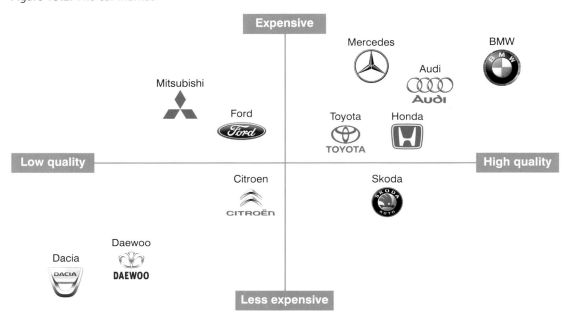

Car makers produce a range of models aimed at different market segments. However, the general position of brands is broadly as indicated. This is a market where attempts to reposition are quite common.

Show your understanding

Using axes of your choice, draw a market map for (a) high street clothing stores and (b) supermarket chains.

Are there any gaps? Are there any potential new markets? Explain your reasoning.

⚠ **WATCH OUT!**

There is often a gap in the market for luxury or high quality products at a low price. This may be because it's not profitable to offer luxury or high quality at a low price; alternatively a low price may damage the luxury image of a product.

Market positioning refers to the way a product is seen in comparison with rival products. Market research helps to position products so that businesses can match customer preferences or appeal to different market segments.

Repositioning means targeting a different market segment, one with more potential sales revenue and/or profit.

A **market map** is a tool that plots brands in the market according to how they meet customers' needs. It allows a business to position individual products effectively.

Competitive advantage

Market positioning and mapping are both aspects of seeking an edge over the competition, making a product stand out. A product which does this has a **competitive advantage**. Apple's iPhone is a good example. This is the main reason for Apple's $18bn (£12bn) profits in the last quarter of 2014, an all-time record. The UK online Apple store currently sells the iPhone 6 for £539, or £619 for the larger version. The estimated profit margin is 40%. Some consumers seem devoted to Apple products.

"The scenes I witnessed at the opening of the new Apple store in London's Covent Garden were more like an evangelical prayer meeting than a chance to buy a phone or a laptop."

Alex Riley, writing for the BBC

Competing effectively

Figure 13.3: Possible routes to gaining competitive advantage

Products often combine more than one of these features. The iPhone 6 has new technology and top notch marketing, but is not sold at a low price and some reviewers have raised issues such as bendiness. Others resent Apple's use of planned obsolescence: changes which make equipment out of date fairly quickly. Being seen as market leader with the best features creates market power, but IBM was market leader in computing a generation ago and is struggling now.

Competitive advantage means having an edge over rival products. There are many ways of making the perception of a product positive, depending on the nature of the market and its consumers.

Product differentiation

**Making the
product
stand out**

Market positioning and competitive advantage are less relevant to commodity products where everyone is selling the same thing. However, there is a grey area here. Unleaded petrol has to conform to strict regulations and have a set quality. Businesses still build brand images in attempts to make their brand seem different and somehow 'better'. Making your offer distinctive can bring advantages.

The major sources of **product differentiation** are:

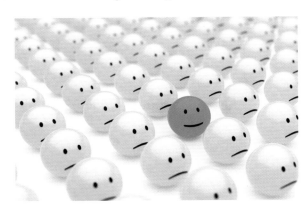

- Differences in quality, usually combined with differences in price.
- Differences in functional features or design.
- Ignorance of buyers about essential features of the product.
- Marketing by sellers, particularly advertising.
- Differences in availability (e.g. timing and location).

The objective of differentiation is to develop a unique image (or a unique selling point, a USP). Being able to stand apart as different brings valuable advantages. Without this, businesses normally have less market power and less profit.

> **Product differentiation** entails unique features which distinguish a product from its rivals. This may be based on special characteristics or a distinct image which has been developed.

Adding value

**Factors of
production**

In order to make a profit a business needs to use the factors of production, land, labour and capital, in such a way that products will sell for more than their total cost. The entrepreneur uses the factors of production to transform the basic material inputs into something that can be sold. This process is called **adding value**.

- Clothing manufacturers add value by transforming fabric, thread, buttons etc. into attractive garments.
- Builders add value to bricks, mortar, girders and glass by assembling them into homes, shops and offices.
- Garden centres might add value by training staff to give gardening advice and offering light refreshments.

Adding value rewards the process of turning inputs into something for which consumers have effective demand at a profitable price. One aspect of this is efficient use of inputs to control costs. Another aspect is ensuring the desirability of products to consumers, which often involves developing an image or design. Or it might mean using better quality inputs, which will be fine if the sales revenue outweighs the costs.

Adding value is easy to understand with physical products where parts are put together to make something useful. Services take more thought, but the principle is the same. Hairdressers frequently take something away, but their inputs create an appearance that consumers want. Value is essentially about consumer perception of 'worth'. We saw earlier that an iPhone 6 is worth more than £500 to many consumers. Adding value leads to a successfully differentiated product with a competitive advantage in a profitable market segment.

> **Adding value** occurs when factors of production are used to make material inputs more valuable to potential customers. It is the difference between the price paid and the total cost of the other inputs needed to create the product.

Pricing decisions

Pricing

Competitive pricing

In a competitive market where products are similar or identical, businesses have little control over pricing. They are driven towards competitive pricing, accepting the market price. If they try to charge more, they will quickly lose out on sales because buyers will be looking to get the best value. Lower prices may increase sales, but rival businesses may make matching price cuts, so that profits are reduced for all. In very competitive markets profits tend to be low anyway, so If this happens there may be a price war and the least efficient businesses may close.

Lidl and Aldi got around this by keeping the quality of products satisfactory while making savings elsewhere. They introduced a lower cost model with basic premises and fewer 'frills' than their rivals. Cutting costs and prices has actually helped them to add value.

This analysis is based on the assumption that markets compete vigorously. In practice, most consumer products are differentiated in some way and competition is about much more than price alone. Good value comes from many sources – quality, design, reliability, convenience and so on. Businesses can aim for a competitive advantage in all the ways mentioned above. Many succeed but in some markets, very big businesses have substantial market power. If there are several very powerful businesses dominating the market, as happens with an oligopoly, price and output decisions will be very much more complicated. You will return to this later in the course.

> **Competitive pricing** takes account of prices charged for similar products competing in the same market. Prices will usually be the same or a little below that of the closest rival.

Stable and dynamic markets

Markets change

Most High Streets have had a branch of WH Smith for a long time. Smith's was the first chain store, with roots in the 18th century. Amongst other things, it retails newspapers which are long established. This looks like a very static situation. Look deeper and the picture changes. WH Smith has been through very difficult times and has had to adapt to survive. Early in this century, it was squeezed between supermarkets that developed overlapping product ranges and specialist book and music stores, both eating into sales. Poor performance led to a takeover bid in 2004 but this fell through. Additional product lines such as toys and confectionery were developed and 70 Post Office branches moved into WH Smith stores in 2007/8.

Changing populations, incomes, tastes and technologies, plus new business ideas, mean that market stability is a relative concept. Few markets stay unchanged for long. The pace of change varies. Stable markets are those which normally change only slowly, whereas dynamic markets keep changing rapidly. Even stable markets encounter shocks, meaning a complacent business can quickly fail.

New technologies

Information and Communications Technology (ICT) has increased the pace of change by speeding up information sharing. The Asus EEE netbook computer went on sale in 2007. Its success encouraged the launch of rival brands and 40 million netbooks were sold. However, the arrival of the iPad and other tablets forced a rapid decline. Asus stopped netbook production in 2011. The nature of tablets is evolving. They might merge with phones into a new standard device, but they might not. Markets for electronic devices are very dynamic. Expansion and collapse can both be very rapid.

Change

Global corporations might seem relatively stable, but this can be an illusion. MacDonald's faces growing competition from rival fast food offerings in many markets. Apple and Samsung (and others) have extended competition into the courts with rival copyright claims. Microsoft, Google and Amazon face increasing pressure from regulators in markets such as the EU, where some of their practices are seen as anti-competitive. Having built a strong position in UK pay TV, Sky now faces pressure from regulators who suspect monopoly powers. It would be a mistake to think that giant businesses are too powerful to fail. Pan American World Airlines went rapidly from one of the world's leading airlines to closure. Polaroid led the world in digital photography for decades, but closed in 2009.

> *"There is nothing permanent except change."*
> Heraclitus, ancient Greek philosopher

Exam style question

Selling the Cactus

Car manufacturing, after many mergers and takeovers, is a global oligopoly. PSA Peugeot Citroen, like many car makers, has struggled with profitability. In 2012 the group lost €5bn. In the first half of 2014, they just reached profitability. They sold almost 3 million cars in 2014, more than half of them in Europe. Capacity is still not fully utilised, with close to 100,000 employees in France, for example. Development costs are high. A new entrant, starting from scratch, would have to spend billions (of £, $ or €) to enter the market. Modifying existing production lines is cheaper but not cheap. It still costs around €500m, even using common components designed for earlier models.

The Cactus shares many parts with the Citroen C3, DS3 and C4, plus a few from Peugeot models. The bodywork is original and 'bold'. Innovations such as 'airbump' panels have been introduced. Its UK starting price is £12,990. Hundreds of thousands must be sold if the Cactus is to be profitable.

Questions

1. What is meant by oligopoly? *(2 marks)*
2. Explain the possible relevance of market mapping to the Cactus. *(4 marks)*
3. Does the Cactus target a market segment or a niche? Explain your answer. *(4 marks)*
4. Discuss ways in which the Cactus might gain competitive advantage. *(8 marks)*
5. Assess likely influences on the pricing strategy for the Cactus. *(12 marks)*

Chapter 14

Why are banks important?

How banks developed

Banking started out in Britain with the medieval goldsmiths: wealthy people needed a safe place to put their gold. So they stored it with the goldsmiths who had safe vaults. After a while, the goldsmiths realised they could make loans to people who wanted to trade or get involved in big construction projects. *The goldsmiths could lend safely because not everyone would need to get their gold back at once.*

Banking really got going in the middle ages in Northern Italy. In the 1340s Edward III was desperately in need of money to fight the 100 Years War in France. He borrowed from the Lombard bankers in Florence. He lost the war and defaulted on the loan – he could not pay the bankers back, and as a result two of them lost everything they had.

By the late 1600s British banks were setting up in Lombard Street in London. Mostly they were small organisations; many were set up by Quakers who were trusted because of their reputation for honesty. Gradually they merged and grew in size and acquired familiar names like Barclays and Lloyds. The connection with Quakers was lost.

The banks' importance in the economy is easily illustrated in this historical context. They were able to accept deposits of gold (and later, cash) from people who wanted to save some of their wealth until they needed it, but required a safe place to store it. They were also able to use that gold (and cash) to finance major projects that neither individuals nor governments could pay for on their own. By charging borrowers (investors) a rate of interest, they made money for themselves and also paid interest to their depositors (savers).

Discussion points

1. Why is it important to be able to raise finance for big projects?
2. Why do governments borrow from the banking system?

Lending and borrowing

Lending is always risky – because like Edward III, borrowers might be unable to repay the loan. That's why banks need to be able to make a profit on the deal, to cover themselves against the risks. But banks also need to be trusted because if they aren't, no one will give them their savings to look after and then they will have nothing much to lend.

Banks rely on the fact that not everyone will want to withdraw their deposits at once. But that only happens if the depositors trust the banks. So the whole banking system is founded on two key factors:

● Banks must act wisely so that they are able to cover the risks they take on when they lend to investors.

● Banks must be trustworthy so that depositors (savers) are confident that their money is safe.

In this respect, nothing much has changed since the middle ages.

> **Banks** take deposits from people and businesses that wish to save and lend to people, businesses and governments that wish to borrow. Operating on a large scale, relying on the fact that not all of their customers will want to withdraw their deposits at once, banks can expand their lending over and above the total amount they receive from savers. This encourages economic growth and helps to raise standards of living.

Providing credit

Why do we want these big projects that require massive amounts of finance? Usually, big projects have to be largely paid for before the products can be sold for cash. We want these projects because they provide us with jobs, incomes, consumer goods, homes and other important things like roads, bridges and hospitals. Sometimes smaller projects are funded by wealthy people or businesses that have made big profits, or by the government, without big bank loans being needed. But usually at least some bank finance is required.

- Exporters need to pay the production costs of the goods they are sending abroad. They require enough money to pay the wages of their employees, the costs of transport to the docks and airports, of getting the goods to their destination and of any other inputs such as raw materials.

- Construction companies similarly need enough money to pay for land, building materials and employees' wages and salaries, up to the time when the building can be sold.

- Businesses need finance for capital equipment.

- All kinds of organisations are likely to need finance, not just businesses that are aiming to make a profit.

Example
Think about the Channel Tunnel. The investment was massive. Some people said, it could never pay for itself. The cost overruns were huge, so big that the banks that financed it had to accept shares instead of straightforward repayment. But life without it is unthinkable now.

Think
You can ponder the London Underground, or indeed the entire railway system., or the drains that keep our cities, villages and homes safe from infections or any of the big, innovative businesses that have changed our lives with their products. They all need finance. Pick one business venture and one infrastructure project and explain why financing it was important.

The role of the banks

If we spent all our money on consumer goods, this whole idea of financing investments would not happen because no one would be saving and there would be no need for a safe place to keep the savings. But what consumer products can we get if we do not invest? We would all have to be hunter gatherers.

Planning a business start-up or buying something big like a house or a car starts with saving because all lenders expect you to contribute some of your own money. You could lend your savings to a friend, on condition that the friend paid you interest and repaid you as soon as you needed the money. Well, you *could*, and you might persuade the friend to give you a better rate of interest than the bank does. But you would be taking a huge risk because by the time you needed the money, the friend might have blown the whole lot on the holiday of a lifetime or lost his job or sunk the money in a failing business venture.

Small savers can never be sure how well an individual borrower is managing their money. Equally, no borrower wants to obtain finance from a number of different individual lenders. Both savers and borrowers need banks.

Show your understanding
I lent my lifetime savings to my sister so she could set up a soft toy making business. Then the economy hit problems and slowed down; I lost my job and toy sales were stagnant. The chances of swift repayment were poor.

In your own words, explain (a) why my action was mistaken, (b) what I should have done and (c) why the outcome would then have been much better for all concerned.

Bank loans

Finance for business

Almost all businesses need bank loans at some time. This may be in order to expand and involve financing of capital equipment. Or the loan may be needed just to cover the costs of production until the sales revenue rolls in.

> **Example**
>
> Hollywell IT Services is a relatively small business which maintains the IT system for a national chain of bakeries. All its customers said, payment will be made 30 days after invoicing, i.e. some time after the work had been done. Long before that, Hollywell would have to pay the rent on the office, wages and salaries and a host of other input costs ranging from equipment to travel. The company needs working capital to cover all these costs, enough to tide them over until the customer pays. Delayed payment is known as trade credit and it is commonly expected, especially by firms that provide services to business.

Many bank loans are made specifically to cover **working capital** needs. Businesses that don't need to borrow every month may go for an overdraft rather than a fixed loan. That means they don't have to pay interest when they don't need the money, but they may have to pay a higher rate of interest for the overdraft facility when they are using it.

> **Working capital** refers to the finance needed to keep the company's day-to-day business going. There must be enough working capital to cover short-term debts.

Paying for credit

> ⚠ **WATCH OUT!**
>
> Don't forget what you learnt on interest rates a while ago. (See Chapter 7, pages 30-31.)

Money doesn't come free. There will be a loan agreement that specifies the interest rate. This may be a fixed rate, or it may vary according to the financial climate and the policy of the central bank (Bank of England).

Interest rates vary according to the level of risk involved. A new business will probably have to pay a higher rate of interest than a well-established business, simply because the bank knows that a high proportion of business start-ups fail. A business with long experience in its field will be much less likely to embark on a project that will not be profitable. Similarly, individuals with a reputation for paying all bills on time will find it easier to get loans at low rates.

A new business will probably have to pay a higher rate of interest for credit.

Collateral

More Magic

Remember Pete and his business, Magic Inspired? (page 21). He had to use his home as collateral for a bank loan. Why?

Well, the business had been going for just four years. It wasn't highly profitable even though it was surviving satisfactorily, so it had not had time to establish a reliable reputation. Pete had put £20,000 of his own money into the business but that wasn't enough to keep the bank happy. So the loan contract said that if he couldn't pay the interest or repay the debt, his house would be sold and the proceeds used to pay back the bank.

Luckily, by getting out before the debts became too big, Pete was able to repay the bank in full. So he didn't lose his home. Using the house as collateral meant that the rate of interest on the loan, at 4%, was fairly reasonable.

Question

How much risk was the bank taking on, in lending to Magic?

A business that owns its premises can use them as collateral with the bank. Mortgage loans work like this too. If you have bought a home with a mortgage and can't pay the interest and the repayments, then the bank will repossess the home and sell it to cover the debts. In both cases, having collateral greatly reduces the risks that the bank is running with these loans.

> **Collateral** on a loan means that there is no risk to the lender. If they cannot be repaid, the collateral assets can be sold to pay off the debt.

Banking regulation

Since the financial crisis in 2008 most governments have tried to constrain their banks, so as to avoid catastrophic bank failures and loss of trust in the banking system. So now banks are expected to be much more careful about lending than they used to be and to avoid lending to too many risky borrowers. You will look at this in more detail later in the course.

Innovation in banking business

Besides acting as intermediaries between lenders and borrowers, banks play a big part in creating an efficient payments system. (You should remember from Chapter 6 that this is important in facilitating specialisation and economic growth.) Thirty years ago everyone used cheques and other paper-based ways of paying, though credit cards were becoming increasingly useful. With ATMs, debit cards and on-line bank transfers, the situation changed completely. But the process of change will not end there. Many in Silicon Valley think that money is just another kind of data, and can be managed by data companies.

Apple, Facebook, Google and Amazon are looking at the possibilities but banks will fight back. Santander is planning to develop various digital services. Payment by phone is already easy but Santander thinks cards will continue to be widely used and cash will not disappear for some time. Clearly banks plan to keep a big share of the payments mechanism, by competing head-on with the data companies.

Find out

Look amongst the news items for the issues that relate to banks right now. In what ways are the banks currently trying to improve their service to customers? Are there some controversial debates relating to the way banks operate? Try to be aware of current issues and consider how changes in the banking system might affect you. For example, at the time of writing it is not easy for young people to get mortgages and become home owners. This situation might improve. Has it? Explain your answer.

Chapter 15

How do banks and businesses cope with risk?

A new B&B

John and Tracy have lived in Margate, a fairly small seaside town on the Kent coast, for years. Margate has until recently suffered from a poor reputation and little investment. Now, however, the town is on the up and is returning to the tourist map. There is a recently built art gallery on the seafront which is helping to attract visitors, especially since an upgraded train service means that they can travel from London in a little over an hour. The local council is also investing money in renovating an historic entertainment venue and investors are buying up cheap local properties.

John and Tracy have a large house on a street near the sea. Their grown-up children have left home and Tracy is considering converting the house into a bed and breakfast business, renting out rooms to tourists and business visitors. Neighbours on local streets have already set up their own businesses, which charge between £40 and £90 per night per room. Tracy is confident that they can make enough money each month so that she can give up her job in the town's tourist office, to be available to look after their guests.

Discussion points

1. Adapting their family home to become a bed and breakfast will cost the couple money, which they will need to borrow from their bank. How might they persuade the bank manager to lend them the money they need?

2. What risks would the bank be running if it decided to lend to the couple?

Spreading risks

Financial intermediaries

The thing that banks do brilliantly is to spread the **risk** associated with lending and borrowing. They act as **financial intermediaries**. The vast majority of the adult population will save for things they want to buy, to provide for their old age or to set up a business. Many people will save small amounts. They want to be sure that their savings are safe and they will deposit them in a bank.

The bank uses the deposits it has received to finance investment. Many of these loans will be quite risky. The bank's function is to keep very careful track of the risks involved and ensure that losses are kept to a minimum. To decide whether to lend to John and Tracy, the bank will require a lot of information about the proposed investment and also a business plan. Among other things, this will need to show how they are going to generate enough business to make some profit.

When losses occur

Then the bank will watch the accounts. Usually if a business looks as if it is going to make significant losses, the bank will 'pull the plug' and insist on speedy repayment. This may well force the business to close down. This will minimise the bank's exposure to likely losses.

Banks also lend to individuals to help them buy cars and homes and sometimes just to provide a personal loan, but they will investigate the customer's credit-worthiness first.

> **Risk:** the possibility that events will not turn out as expected. The probability of some risks can be calculated, by referring to past experience, but mistakes may be made and uncertainty may make calculation impossible.
>
> **Financial intermediaries** include retail and investment banks, building societies, pension funds and insurance companies. They all offer a link between investors and savers.

Evaluating risk

Banks have to understand the risks they are running before they offer loans.

Spreading risks

- First of all, a bank needs to have a wide range of borrowers just so that if any one of them becomes a business failure, it is not a disaster for the bank. Others will succeed. For this reason, small banks have sometimes in the past been at a disadvantage.

- Some risks can be quantified. A range of possible outcomes can be studied and for some, probabilities can be identified.

- Banks gain experience over time and can assess the likelihood of misfortune on the basis of the information they have about the borrower.

Investment banks

- Some banks specialise in particular types of lending, and gain expertise in that field. Investment banks typically lend to substantial businesses. This is especially helpful where large loans are needed and makes it possible to organise a consortium of banks for really big projects. Retail banks are likely to have many small business borrowers.

- Banks lend to each other, to cover surpluses and deficits that are a consequence of day-to-day payments. These loans are typically very short-term, maybe just overnight. This helps banks to keep going through short-term fluctuations in day-to-day payments.

A juggling act

Profits for banks

There is a tradeoff between risk and safety. Risky loans are often more profitable, because a higher rate of interest can be charged. So banks do like to make some risky business loans, in the hope of a big profit. On the other hand, if they make too many loans for risky ventures, they may find that they are losing money when things go wrong.

You may have noticed that credit card loans usually involve a very high rate of interest, up to 20% sometimes. No special arrangement is needed and this kind of loan is quite likely to be used by people who are in difficulty and would struggle to get any other kind of loan. There is a significant risk that the credit card company will have difficulty getting full repayment; the higher interest rate compensates them for the high risk factor.

How do businesses deal with risk?

What businesses must do

Entrepreneurs need to consider very carefully how they are going to ensure that they succeed with their business venture. They must understand their market, have good ideas, know about potential competitors and be prepared to work hard. They may find it helpful to draw up a business plan. The flow chart shows how a business might try to minimise risks.

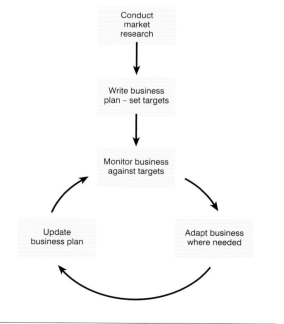

Unlimited liability

Sole traders

It is really easy to set up a business with **unlimited liability**; an entrepreneur who does this will be described as a sole trader. All that needs to be done is to inform HMRC (Her Majesty's Revenue and Customs) that the business exists and to keep accurate records of the business income and expenses. At the end of each tax year the sole trader must complete a tax return and pay tax on their income. They must also pay National Insurance contributions.

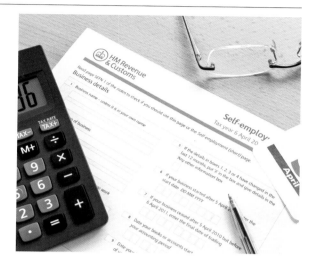

The difficulty is that if anything goes wrong the sole trader will have to repay all the debts that have been incurred. They will have to use their own money to do this and if they do not have enough cash to cover all the debts, their possessions and property can be used to make the necessary repayments. Legally, the sole trader and the business are one and the same.

Examples

An artist or an author may be self employed in this way and function perfectly well, working from home. Their costs of production may be just paints and canvases for the artist and maybe a computer for the author. They will probably not incur significant debts and so this will be a safe course of action. Of course they may not make much money, because success depends on talent and popularity, but they cannot avoid that risk.

Business risks

But supposing the business is a camera shop, and costs include rent for the premises, wages for the staff, business rates and payments for a varied stock of cameras (though the manufacturers may be prepared to wait for that). By the time the entrepreneur realises that camera sales are down because people are using mobile phones and the shop will never be profitable, the debts may have mounted up very seriously. If the owner has unlimited liability the debts might be very hard to deal with.

Think

This scenario could be quite discouraging for an entrepreneur. Why might we not want entrepreneurs always to have unlimited liability for their debts?

Limited liability

Private limited companies

Most small businesses register from the start as **private limited companies** (with Ltd. after the company name). This makes the business into a separate legal entity that is distinct from the owner and any other shareholders. Once the business is registered at Companies House it will be subject to company law. The entrepreneur and any other shareholders will put money into the business to get it started. If debts build up this money can be used to make necessary repayments but the shareholders cannot be required to use their own personal assets to cover the debts. They can only lose the money they have already put into the business. They are said to have **limited liability**.

Shareholders

This approach reduces the risks involved in setting up a business. Owners will sell shares only to people they know. In exchange for part ownership of the business the entrepreneur can raise significant finance for investment. In return the shareholders will receive part of the business profit in the form of dividends.

Some shareholders may want to have an input into how the business is run while others may be happy to receive their dividend without having any regular contact with the business.

There are more regulations governing private limited companies than there are for sole traders. These will increase the cost and complexity of administration in running the business. But this is offset by limited liability and easier access to finance.

Sole traders	Private limited companies
Advantages	**Advantages**
Full control of the business. Owner receives all profit.	Limited liability for business debts. Easier to get bank loans.
Disadvantages	**Disadvantages**
Unlimited liability for all debts. Can be hard to raise finance	More regulation. Sharing the profits. Shareholder involvement.

PLCs

Public limited companies also have limited liability but issue shares to the general public and are governed by many more regulations than private limited companies. This is not an option for entrepreneurs when setting up a business since the initial share offering must raise at least £50,000. (This is highly unlikely for a business with no trading history.) Public limited companies must publish their financial accounts each year – you can read the accounts of many well-known businesses by searching through their websites to find the pages where this information is published.

Find out
Use the website www.businesslink.gov.uk to find out more about the processes involved in setting up different types of business organisation.

Unlimited liability means that an individual has no legal separation from their business and is therefore personally responsible for the debts of the business. Their personal assets could be used to pay business debts if the business is not able to cover them.

Limited liability protects shareholders in that as individuals they are legally separate from the business. The most that shareholders have to contribute towards business debts is the amount of capital originally invested in buying shares.

The owners of **private limited companies** have limited liability for business debts but cannot raise finance from the general public. They are often family businesses and the shareholders are members of the family or personal friends. They are usually small or medium-sized businesses.

Public limited companies (**PLCs**) are owned by their shareholders, who have limited liability. The companies can raise finance by selling shares to the general public and large organisations such as pension funds. In this way they can raise substantial finance in order to expand.

Why limited liability is important

According to Bloomburg, 80% of business start-ups fail within 18 months. Of course some of these will have been temporary in nature anyway but the fact remains that new businesses are very vulnerable. Without limited liability many promising entrepreneurs with good ideas would simply not take the risk. That would mean that some potentially viable businesses which could be creating useful products and valued jobs would never see the light of day. Small businesses can grow fast and be of great benefit to society and the economy. Limited liability helps to create positive opportunities.

Chapter 16

How do businesses find the finance they need?

A business start-up

Thomas Jones was 27 when he set up his business, selling educational software. To start with, a small investor took an interest and was prepared to back him. But when friends and family heard about it they too wanted to play a part in the start-up; together they raised enough money to get the business going. Some bought shares and some provided loans.

At the end of the first year, sales revenue was still much less than hoped. Thomas could not make enough to live on, leave alone pay back some of the loans. He reduced the number of staff and got a job working for someone else. He had to tell his backers, both friends and family members. He had always warned them that start-ups often fail but he still felt bad about it.

For a while, the business ticked over on a low level, surviving but making no profit. Thomas continued to manage the business in his spare time. The backers were remarkably faithful; perhaps they had thought things through carefully and decided before getting involved that they could afford to lose the money they had lent. Then an opportunity arose – Facebook backed the company to create a related product as an app. The shareholders can't yet sell their shares to get their money back but they will be able to soon, if all goes well.

Discussion points

1. When might friends and family be the best source of finance?
2. What risks were the investors taking when they financed the start-up?

External vs. internal finance

Sources of finance

The angel investor who took an interest in Thomas Jones' business at the outset, and Facebook later on, provided **external finance**, as did the friends and family who bought shares and gave loans. This kind of finance is often very appropriate for a new start-up. Well-established businesses that are ready to expand are more likely to use **internal finance**. Businesses need to think carefully about which sources of finance will be most appropriate for them.

Figure 16.1

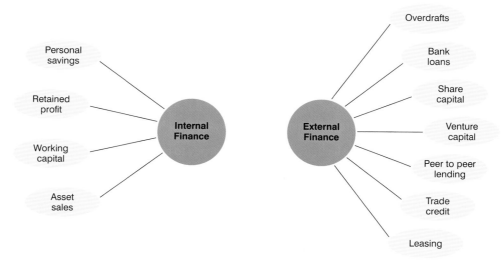

Internal sources of finance

- **Personal savings:** many entrepreneurs make considerable efforts to save for themselves as a way of financing a start-up or expansion. Banks are usually impressed if part of the cost can be covered by the owner and may be more likely to provide additional loan finance as a result.

- **Retained profit:** once a business is operational it should be generating revenue. So long as total costs are lower than total revenue, there will be some profit. This profit can either be taken out of the business by the owners, as a reward for their enterprise, or can be retained and reinvested in the business. Retained profit can also be kept in order to cover unexpected cost overruns.

- **Sale of assets:** an asset is something of value. In a business this could refer to physical resources such as vans, machines, buildings, land or stocks, or it could be something less tangible such as a successful brand or a patent for a particular technical design. Any asset can be sold to generate cash to cover business costs.

- **Working capital:** this refers to cash that the business can access immediately. (It may have come from retained profits.) It is available to cover immediate costs that must be paid for ahead of the time when sales revenue flows in.

> **Internal finance** comes from within the business. It can be *retained profit* or cash raised from the *sale of assets*.
>
> **Personal saving** is an important source of finance for new or small businesses. Before getting started, the entrepreneur will save in order to fund the early expenses associated with the production process. It may also contribute to the purchase of capital equipment.
>
> **Retained profit** is profit that is being reinvested in the business rather than being given to the owner(s) of the business in the form of dividend payments. It does not incur interest payments or dilute ownership of the business. It is a long-term source of finance.
>
> The **sale of assets** can refer to physical assets such as machinery or property, or to intangible assets such as the patent to a particular product. It is a long-term source of finance.
>
> **Working capital** is cash held by the business and used to keep day-to-day business going in the short run.

External sources of finance

External finance comes from individuals or organisations which are not part of the business. These investors may offer finance in exchange for **equity**. Equity finance gives the business money in return for a **share** of the business. This money does not have to be paid back. In a private limited company, shareholders will be limited to people known to the entrepreneur.

Occasionally it is possible for an entrepreneur to get a *grant*, i.e. finance that neither has to be paid back nor involves giving up ownership of any of the business. The government and certain charities, such as the Prince's Trust, offer grants to some small business start-ups. These organisations may also provide low-interest loans to entrepreneurs that meet their criteria.

A previously private limited company that is ready to go public, i.e. become a PLC, can raise large amounts of **ordinary share capital** by organising an IPO (initial public offering). Well-established PLCs can also create and sell shares; this is useful for companies that need finance for the development of a new product or market expansion. PLC shareholders can sell their shares on the **Stock Exchange** when they wish to.

(margin labels: Retained profit; Equity finance; PLCs)

	For	Against
Share capital	Share capital does not have to be paid back and does not incur interest. Shares in PLCs can be sold on the Stock Exchange – this may encourage investors.	The original owner of the business gives up some control over it as shareholders must be consulted. In time, new shareholders will expect to receive dividends as a reward for investing, so the original owner will receive less profit in the future.

Share capital

Venture capital

Venture capital is a form of long-term equity finance; an investor provides money for the business in exchange for a share of its ownership. Entrepreneurs generally seek venture capital when they are unable to raise the money needed through other channels, since giving up ownership of the business reduces their control over the business. It also means that any future profits will have to be shared. Venture capitalists are willing to take greater risks than other lenders so may be used when banks refuse to lend. Venture capitalists may offer advice and support to entrepreneurs as well as their financial investment. Some will demand a say in how the business is run. All will expect dividends, in time.

External finance comes from banks or investors that have no direct connection with the company.

Ordinary share capital is long-term finance raised by selling shares in a business. Share capital does not have to be repaid. Investors receive part-ownership of the business and a share of the profits in the form of dividends.

Equities: another name for shares.

Stock Exchange: a market where shares in PLCs can be bought and sold. Investors can sell if for some reason they need the money they invested.

Venture capital is money invested in a new business by one or more individuals who believe that the business will succeed and therefore increase in value, but are willing to accept the risk that the business idea may fail. Venture capitalists may offer advice and technical support as well as finance. Venture capital is long-term and may be provided in exchange for a share of the equity of a business.

Bank finance

Loans

Loans are one of the commonest forms of external finance. The business borrows a fixed sum of money for a fixed period of time, making fixed regular repayments. The lender will demand *interest* as their reward for lending the money. Entrepreneurs may seek loans from a bank, or from willing family or friends.

The rate of interest will depend on a number of factors including:

● the current Bank of England interest rate.
● the size of the loan.
● the repayment period.
● whether the lender perceives a significant risk of the business defaulting on the loan (i.e. not paying it back).

Overdrafts are short-term loans offered by banks. An overdraft allows a business to spend more money than is available in the business bank account. Effectively, an overdraft is an agreement to let the bank balance become negative. Interest is calculated daily on the overdrawn balance, usually at a rate higher than that charged for a fixed loan.

A **loan** is an amount of money borrowed for a fixed period at a fixed interest rate. The loan is paid back in regular instalments until the total amount plus interest is repaid. Loans are medium- to long-term sources of finance.

An **overdraft** is a short-term flexible loan where a bank allows a business to operate with a negative bank balance. Interest is paid on the amount overdrawn, usually at a higher rate than is charged for a fixed sum loan. Overdrafts are useful for covering short term debt.

	For	**Against**
Loans	High Street banks may see well-established businesses as low risk and give low-interest loans. For business start-ups, family or friends of the business owners may provide finance, which is helpful if banks are unwilling to lend to an entrepreneur with no security and no trading history.	The higher the perceived risk, the higher the interest rate. New businesses may find it hard to get a loan from a bank at a low rate. Lenders may require collateral. If the business cannot repay the loan, the lender can sell the asset to recover their money. The most commonly secured assets are buildings; they reduce the risks on long-term loans.
Overdrafts	Overdrafts can be used to borrow a flexible amount for a short time. As soon as money is deposited in the business account, it reduces the overdraft balance.	A bank is able to cancel an overdraft at any time and request full repayment. The interest rate on an overdraft is variable so an increase in the Bank of England interest rate can be passed on quickly.

Overdrafts

Example
The television programme Dragons' Den is based around venture capital. The Dragons are all venture capitalists who decide whether they are willing to risk investing their money in new business ideas. On the programme you can see negotiations between the Dragons and entrepreneurs where they decide how much money will be invested in exchange for a specific share of ownership of the business.

Leasing

Leasing is used by businesses that need land, buildings or equipment which they are unable or unwilling to buy outright. It is the name given to 'renting' an asset. Many businesses lease vehicles, or office equipment such as photocopiers, or office space.

	For	**Against**
Leasing	Leasing is a more flexible way to acquire an asset than outright purchase. Leasing can be used for long-term or short-term finance.	The business never takes ownership of the item. The business will pay more than the market value of the leased items in the long term.

Trade credit

Trade credit is short-term finance offered to a business by suppliers. It means the business can obtain the inputs it needs and pay for them later, when sales revenue is coming in. Trade credit is typically offered for 30 to 60 days, though it may be possible for a business to bargain for a longer credit period. In times of financial difficulty a supplier may shorten the credit period or limit the total credit offered because they themselves are short of cash.

Example

A bakery needs supplies of flour, butter and sugar in order to produce cakes for sale. The bakery bank account has a balance of £0 so there is no money available to pay for the supplies immediately. The bank has refused an overdraft on the account. Luckily, the supplier allows 30 days trade credit. This means that the bakery can receive the raw materials without having to pay for them and has time to bake and sell cakes, receiving revenue from these sales, and paying the supplier before the end of the 30 day credit period.

Leasing allows a business to use an asset without owning it, by making regular payments to the owner of the asset. Over time the total sum paid for the lease may be more than the cost of buying the asset outright.

Trade credit is a short-term source of finance offered when suppliers allow a time period before payment for supplies must be made. The credit period will vary between suppliers and may be changed by the supplier at any time.

Individual investors

By-passing banks

An individual venture capital investor has to be capable of finding a business and assessing the risks involved in investing. Different people have different levels of risk aversion. Direct investment is only for those who can assess the risk and survive if the worst happens. Many direct investors will join a fund of some kind so that they can spread the risks by investing in a range of different companies.

There are many new and innovative investment businesses; between 2010 and 2014, 25 new venture capital funds were established in London. These have developed as more investors wanted to invest directly in promising looking businesses, many of which are start-ups. The action is largely concentrated in technology products but could soon spread to other types of business.

Collaborative funding

Working online, investors can gather information about businesses that are looking for finance. They can contribute relatively small amounts to a range of individual businesses, knowing that it is unlikely that all their investments will end in losses.

Examples

Collaborative Fund runs AngelList, a list of companies seeking finance. Initially it specialised in gaming start-ups but that is changing. Dealflicks is on the list; it helps sell empty cinema seats in the USA at a discount of up to 60%, when the cinemas know they have unsold seats. Together the investors raised $1.8 million during 2014. In early 2015, Collaborative set up a similar scheme for UK investors and businesses.

Peer-to-peer lending

Peer-to-peer (aka P2P) lending platforms function like marketplaces where lenders can connect with borrowers. In 2014, they raised £1.2 billion in loans for UK businesses. The government created one such platform, Funding Circle. It is backed by the British Business Bank, a government-owned financial intermediary. It reckons to get investors a rate of return (from interest on loans) of around 7%, after allowing for potential losses and service charges.

Choosing a source of finance

The objectives of the owner will influence choice of finance.

● Some entrepreneurs would prefer to retain full control of their business so take out loans rather than give up equity in their business.

Selecting a source of finance

● Others are uncomfortable with the notion of being in debt or don't want the stress of meeting repayment deadlines. In this case equity finance may be a better choice than borrowing.

● Entrepreneurs whose primary objective is growth may not be willing to wait for enough retained profit to fund expansion, preferring to raise external finance in order to achieve their objective more quickly.

> ### ⚠ WATCH OUT!
>
> Whilst retained profit is often the preferred source of finance for a business, simply stating that 'this business should use retained profit to fund this venture' would be simplistic. Remember that all choices incur a *trade-off* of some kind. The use of retained profit assumes, of course, that the business has sufficient profit available to it, but it also means that the entrepreneur cannot benefit personally by receiving the profit in the form of dividends. If this does not suit the *objectives* of the owners at the time, retained profit will be an inappropriate source of finance.

Credit and the economy

Will investment increase?

Job creation and prosperity generally require entrepreneurial flair and steady investment. Business dynamism requires some optimism about demand for the product. Perhaps this is one reason why recent new investment strategies tend to focus on technology-related start-ups.

From 2008 until 2013, business optimism was very muted because of the financial crisis and subsequent recession, involving low levels of consumer demand. However, a whole range of businesses expressed an intention to invest more in 2014. Many banks may remain rather cautious about lending, perhaps for several years, and this may starve businesses of the credit that would allow them to invest and expand. However, as of early 2015, many businesses have a considerable amount of retained profit which may finance an increase in investment, if demand for consumer products is growing.

Find out and show your understanding
1. Is there news in the press of businesses having difficulty in accessing bank credit in order to expand?
2. Have government expenditure cuts caused reduced levels of demand for some products? If so, how has this affected business plans to invest?
3. What can recent data tell us about current levels of investment?

Exam style question

Carol and Richard Faulkner have a love of food and of cooking. For many years they have talked about opening up their own restaurant and now they are finally doing it. They have taken out a 12-month lease on a site in their local town centre, furnished it in a simple, homely style and chosen a menu that is getting very positive feedback from customers so far.

Both Carol and Richard gave up well-paid jobs in order to start the restaurant. Although they are currently living on the last of their savings, neither regrets it. They are enjoying the excitement of running a new business and the freedom which comes from being their own boss. They are hoping that the restaurant will break even in the next six months and be profitable by the end of the year.

Questions
1. What is meant by 'lease'? *(2 marks)*
2. Explain the main advantage of leasing rather than buying premises for a restaurant. *(4 marks)*
3. Explain the opportunity cost to Carol and Richard of opening their restaurant. *(4 marks)*
4. Discuss **two** possible reasons for a high failure rate of restaurant start-ups. *(8 marks)*
5. Assess Carol and Richard's decision to fund their start-up with their savings and a bank loan rather than borrow from friends and family. *(12 marks)*

Chapter 17

What happens when markets fail?

Mrs Walker

Mrs Walker's house backed onto the site of a medium sized secondary school. Noise and bustle at the start and end of the school day, and at breaks, became an accepted part of her daily routine. There was a basketball court in the playground on her side of the school. Groups of young people began playing basketball on the court during summer evenings. The head teacher had no objection, no damage was done apart from some litter and he saw basketball as a positive and healthy activity. For Mrs Walker it was too much. The persistent noise of bouncing balls invaded her evening peace and occasional shouting upset her.

Eventually, the local authority ordered the school to stop the noise, on environmental health grounds. With no effective fencing, the school finally took the basketball rings off the backboards to end the nuisance.

Discussion points

1. Each of the parties in this situation had rights. Explain what these were in each case.
2. The outcome involved both costs and benefits. Who did they each affect, and in what way?

Externalities

In deals between economic agents, typically a seller and a buyer, there are two sides. Sometimes an activity has 'spillover' effects which have consequences for someone else, a **third party**. These spillover effects are called **externalities**. If such spillover effects are negative, we call them an external cost. The noisy basketball games became an external cost to Mrs Walker. We most often focus on **external costs** from production, such as pollution.

Example

One of the worst examples of external costs came in Bhopal, India, back in 1984. Toxic gases escaped from a pesticide factory. This caused thousands of deaths and around 250,000 serious medical conditions. An estimated 700,000 people suffered some external costs.

Externalities are not all bad. Sometimes we benefit from other people's activity. For example, successful immunisation programmes can lead to big reductions in the risk of catching diseases. Polio was a very serious illness, causing paralysis to 1,000 children a day in 1988. Since then, 2.5 billion children have been immunised worldwide. Reported cases have fallen to little more than one a day. Just three countries still have some polio, due to a mix of instability, conflict, isolation and poor infrastructure. The chance of having polio passed on to us is virtually zero in almost the entire world. Even if people are not themselves immunised, nobody can pass polio on to them. They gain an **external benefit** from this reduced risk.

Private costs and benefits

A weakness of the free market system is that it ignores external costs and benefits. Output at the equilibrium level depends on the benefit from the product shown by the demand curve, together with the cost of producing. How much people will pay (shown by the demand curve) shows us how much **private benefit** or 'welfare' they expect to gain from consumption. Supplying is only worthwhile if the price covers the cost to producers. This cost is their **private cost** because they are only concerned with the costs they have to pay. This system takes no account of external costs or external benefits.

A **third party** is someone other than the buyer or seller who experiences the consequences of others' economic activity.

Externalities are costs or benefits that affect anyone other than the buyer or seller, i.e. all third parties.

External costs are costs which impact on third parties.

External benefits are gains which impact on third parties.

Private benefits are a buyer's gains from consumption of goods and services.

Private costs are the costs paid by a supplier of a good or service.

Think
Describe one external cost that you personally have experienced, and one social benefit.

Social costs

Social costs may exceed private costs

From an overall perspective, activities are worthwhile if the total benefits created (including any external benefits) are greater than the total costs (including any external costs). To check this, we add together private and external benefits, calling the combined total **social benefits**. If this is greater than the **social costs** (of private plus external costs), an activity is worthwhile. We can modify supply and demand diagrams to include externalities. A standard supply curve shows private costs; firms will only want to supply their product if these costs are covered. When there are external costs, we can add these to the private costs to show social costs, as in Figure 17.1.

Figure 17.1: External costs

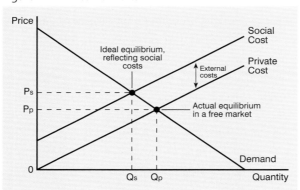

If there are significant social costs, the free market equilibrium (at Q_p and P_p) produces more than is ideal. We can see that for the last unit produced the social cost is more than the benefit as shown by demand.

Over-production

Over-consumption

Large factory-fishing ships, equipped with high technology, can quickly scoop up much of the fish stock in areas of sea. The price they get justifies the costs they pay. Local fishermen with smaller boats have an external cost when less is left for them to catch, especially if fish stocks drop below a sustainable level and go into long term decline. Cutting activity back to the level (Q_s), where benefits match social costs, is better for everyone except the owners of factory-fishing ships, who maximise their short term profits and then move away elsewhere. External costs are associated with **overproduction** or **overconsumption**.

Social costs are the total of private costs and any external costs.

Social benefits are the total of private benefits and any external benefits.

Overproduction or **overconsumption** occur when prices reflect only the private costs of production, ignoring the external costs.

⚠ WATCH OUT!

Many people confuse social costs with external costs. It is important to be clear that social costs refer to *both* private and external costs added together. Where there are external costs they will be less than social costs. Choose the right words carefully.

Social benefits

Social benefit may exceed private benefit

Where there are external benefits, we can add them to the private benefits by shifting the demand curve upwards as shown below.

Figure 17.2: External benefits

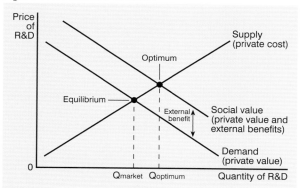

Graduates tend to be more productive, to earn more and to pay more tax. A highly educated and skilled workforce can be expected to create a larger national output than less able workers could. Higher output brings external benefits for the whole community. For example, the government can provide better public sector services if it wishes to. This means that the social benefit of university education is greater than the private benefit.

If students (or their families) pay fees to cover the cost of university education, the market equilibrium could be shown at quantity Q_{market} on Figure 17.2. The social optimum output is $Q_{optimum}$. This is where the benefit from educating the last student just matches the cost. In a free market system, fewer people will go into higher education than would be optimal for society, unless there is some kind of intervention. The difference will be the gap between Q_{market} and $Q_{optimum}$. There may be **underproduction** of graduates.

Under-production

Low interest student loans can be seen as one type of intervention, especially when the system is structured so that many students will never repay all of their debt. Some people argue that fees should be scrapped and that everyone capable of reaching degree standard should have the chance to go to university. Others think that that is too costly for society.

Show your understanding
Identify two situations (other than those mentioned above) where consumer choices involve products that create external costs and one situation where external benefits occur. Identify the gainers and the losers in each situation and explain what is happening.

The market, choices and efficiency

We have seen that scarcity and choice are central to economics. We don't have the resources to produce everything we want, so we must choose between alternatives. The free market system allows people to choose how to use their limited incomes. Every time we spend, we effectively vote for resources to go into

Profit signalling mechanism

what we buy. Firms will supply all that can be sold for a profitable price. If we don't want something enough to pay a profitable price, it will not be produced and resources will not be wasted. The profit signalling mechanism encourages efficient use of resources.

Shifts in tastes and in technology lead to demand and supply changes, so prices and market signals do change. This system adjusts automatically, far more simply than having an army of bureaucrats taking all the decisions about what should be made and how to make it.

Example

At the start of this century, many people had personal CD players which they used with headphones. The Sony Walkman was the market leader. MP3 players with flash memory came along, offering more capacity and versatility in a smaller machine. These advantages meant that demand for personal CD players slumped and firms stopped producing them, Sony switched the Walkman brand to MP3 players. Now, many people prefer to store their music on a smartphone, so few resources are going into MP3 players.

Competition reduces waste

Besides signalling how resources should be used, the market system can bring other benefits. We assume that firms are motivated by profits and want to maximise them. Minimising production costs increases profit. In other words, firms have an incentive not to waste any resources in order to keep costs low. Innovation becomes very attractive to firms in competitive industries because offering consumers a new and better product frequently leads to more sales and profits. Innovation in production methods can also reduce costs. Fear of being undercut by competitors' prices brings pressure on competing firms to keep prices low and to give consumers the best possible service.

Market failure

Unfortunately, theoretical market models are based on assumptions that cannot be relied upon. They ignore realities that can reduce the efficiency of market resource allocation. We call the outcome **market failure**.

How markets fail

Market fail for many reasons. The four main ones are:

- When external costs harm third parties, these costs will not be reflected in the price of the product. People will buy more than they would if the price was based on the social cost. There will be over-production and overconsumption.

- The price mechanism only works efficiently if there is genuine competition between producers. In some sectors of the economy, businesses may have some market power. By producing less, they can push up the price of the product. Buyers will pay more for it than they would in a competitive market.

- Some important products, e.g. health care, will not be provided by the market system in adequate quantities to meet the need of everyone, including those who cannot pay.

- When there is insufficient information about products, buyers may select an inferior product or one with a price that is higher than the costs of production.

> **Underproduction** and **underconsumption** occur when less is produced than would be optimal for society as a whole, given the external benefits of the product.
>
> **Market failure** occurs when markets allocate resources inefficiently, often because market prices are distorted. Governments may intervene to correct market failure, using anti-monopoly legislation or provision of public services or regulating industries that create external costs.

Competition

Example

Petrol and diesel distributors were slow to cut prices in late 2014 despite falling world prices for oil. They did not seem interested in price competition. The Chief Secretary to the Treasury (Danny Alexander) wrote to them asking them to cut prices. Competition needed at least a nudge. Reality often fails to match the theory and markets can fail to work efficiently.

Exam style question

The Interoceanic Highway

The Interoceanic Highway is a 5,500 kilometres long route reaching right across South America. It cuts through The Amazonian rainforest which is the largest area of its type in the world. Social benefits include lower costs for farmers and businesses, and can make a difference between life and death for people in remote areas far from hospitals. Land speculators, loggers, farmers, ranchers, gold miners and others can profit from exploiting opportunities along the route.

Externalities

As the highway crosses the Peruvian Amazon region, a discreet sign urges travellers to protect the surrounding ecosystem. "Let's care for the environment, let's conserve the forest" it reads. When the road was constructed, tall trees lined the route. The forest edge now lies about half a kilometre away, beyond a jumble of underbrush and freshly cut trees where a cattle pasture was recently carved out of the woods. As drivers head east into Brazil, the view is much the same for hundreds of kilometres. A study by South Dakota State University found that 95% of deforestation in the region occurs within 7 kilometres of a road. Rapid deforestation early in this century was followed by a lull, but today the rainforests are being destroyed by 1.5 acres every second. Since 1978, over 750,000 square kilometres of Amazon rainforest have been destroyed. Once cleared, the soil is of such low quality that it can hardly be used to grow anything. After a year or two of farming, the land is totally stripped of nutrients – leaving a useless patch of ground.

Tropical rainforests only cover just 6% of the Earth's surface, but are home to more than half the world's plant and animal species and bring extensive external benefits. Around 80% of the foods we eat originally came from rainforests. Over a quarter of the medicines we use have their origins in the rainforests. With deforestation, 137 rainforest species (mainly plants) are exterminated completely every day. Roads cause drying which influences local atmospheric circulation patterns and can also contribute to global warming by releasing carbon stored in the forest.

Adapted from Nature.com, *The Guardian*, 19 October 2014, Rainforests.mongabay.com and Onthegotours.com.

Questions

1. What is meant by 'external benefits' (paragraph 2)?   *(2 marks)*
2. Briefly explain private benefits from The Interoceanic Highway.   *(4 marks)*
3. Explain one economic reason why deforestation mainly occurs close to roads.   *(4 marks)*
4. Discuss the external costs of deforestation.   *(8 marks)*
5. Assess the extent to which the Interoceanic Highway illustrates market failure.   *(12 marks)*

Chapter 18

Government intervention and failure

Tobacco

Tobacco kills people. Cancer Research UK tells us that it kills tens of thousands of people each year in the UK and over 5 million worldwide. It is the single biggest cause of avoidable cancer in the world. Around half of regular smokers will be killed by the habit. In addition to the damage they do themselves, smokers impose damage (external costs) on people around them via passive smoking. Despite the efforts of tobacco companies to question these facts, the scientific evidence is beyond dispute.

There are still defenders of smoking, organised by groups such as FOREST. "Tobacco is not an illegal substance yet the government is persecuting a minority. I think that's a disgrace in a social democracy" said playwright Sir Ronald Harwood. Rather than thinking in terms of persecution, governments feel a duty to intervene in order to protect their populations from tobacco damage. There are laws against children buying tobacco and against smoking in public places (even in bars). There are bans on many forms of tobacco advertising. There are heavy taxes on tobacco products. New restrictions are often in the pipeline. Campaigns to help smokers break the habit are subsidised. At the time of writing, both insistence on plain packaging and a ban on smoking in cars are being considered. There is progress. A generation ago (1980) around 45% of UK adults smoked; the current figure is below 25%. However, there are still young people laying foundations for a lifelong tobacco addiction.

Discussion points

1. Do you agree that smokers are persecuted?

2. Drivers, and any passengers, get concentrated doses of damaging smoke and chemicals from smoking in cars. Does this fact justify a ban?

3. What would happen if tobacco was simply made an illegal substance?

Market forces and government controls

A free market economy is one in which market forces determine the way in which resources are allocated. We have seen that this works well when strong competition encourages businesses to keep production costs as low as possible. But the market economy does not guarantee that everyone will have a reasonable standard of living. This is one aspect of market failure; others can be seen wherever there are external costs.

Market failure

Governments try to deal with market failure. They have a range of intervention strategies, but success is not always guaranteed. One option, where there is underproduction, is public sector provision (e.g. of health care). Instead of relying on market forces, governments keep control of things they regard as too important to be left to the free market. The extreme case occurs where there is a **command economy** and all economic activity is in the public sector. The best remaining example is probably North Korea, where the government still makes most decisions on what is produced and how.

Mixed economies

Mixed economies are now the norm. Much is left to private enterprise and market forces but government controls policing, defence and usually education and health services for most of the population.

> A **command economy** relies predominantly on public sector provision of goods and services.
>
> **Mixed economies** have a private sector and a public sector. They are market economies with significant public sector activity, where decisions are based on the public interest.

Private vs. public sectors

Supporters of the private sector believe that free markets create efficiency which public sectors cannot match. The profit motive pressurises private firms to minimise costs. Public sector managers may be paid according to the size of their budgets or the number of their employees. With no requirement for profit, they have an incentive to spend more and employ more people, which is inefficient. There are examples of efficient public sector activities, with or without market incentives. You need not look far to find examples of nurses, teachers or police officers going far beyond the call of duty, for example. Inefficient private sector firms are also common, especially where there is little competition.

However, dislike of paying taxes and suspicion of public sector waste lead to accusations of **government failure** and calls for more reliance on the market system.

Government failure

> **Government failure** occurs when a public sector activity or government intervention, intended to correct a market failure, makes the situation worse rather than better.

Think

Governments intervene, (a) to reduce smoking and (b) to raise the incomes of people living below the poverty line. In each case, consider what is the nature of the market failure? Is there any evidence of government failure?

Competition

Late in the last century, privatisation shifted utilities and services from the public to the private sector in many countries, with the most spectacular results in China. In the UK, some privatisations proved more successful than others. BT quickly shed workers once privatised, with no apparent reduction in service quality. Elsewhere, as with water or many rail franchises, results have been more mixed. The pressure to operate efficiently is far less without competition and privatised monopolies have needed regulation to control their market power.

Legislation and regulation

Harmful products can be banned by law, as with dangerous drugs. Governments may take different approaches: codeine is freely available in painkillers in many countries, but is banned in the United Arab Emirates as it is derived from opium. Many weapons are banned from individual ownership, to protect both the individual and society. Some bans protect the environment and wildlife.

Changing behaviour

Alongside bans, **regulation** is common. Many countries regulate tobacco advertising, sale and use, to deter smokers and to protect non-smokers. Regulations on vehicle use aim to reduce road accidents. Other regulations aim at protecting the environment; these vary between countries. Regulations are not all prohibitive. For example, they enforce school attendance; in some countries voting is compulsory.

If we ban hard drugs or driving without seat belts, does this infringe liberties and force us into a 'nanny state'? A powerful lobby in the USA defends 'the right to bear arms' as a fundamental freedom. Ultimately, bans depend on broad public support in order to succeed. Laws are only effective if enforced. For example, the ban on smoking in bars is largely respected in the UK now that the dangers are appreciated. However, using phones whilst driving is dangerous, yet enforcement seems weak. There are limits to the extent to which people can be protected from themselves and others.

Think

Why do people do things which harm themselves and others?

Is education as important as legislation if we want to change behaviour?

'Red-tape' – the costs of compliance and bureaucracy, make business harder and less profitable.

Regulation

Regulation is seen by many as a 'burden on business', and very damaging. Costs of compliance and bureaucracy ('red tape') are seen to make business harder and less profitable. On the other hand, lack of building regulation enforcement allowed the accumulation of heavy garment machinery in a multi-storey building in Dacca, Bangladesh, and then hundreds of deaths when the building collapsed. Regulations on working conditions, health & safety and fair treatment of workers can be a costly nuisance for employers, but improve the quality of life for employees. There is a trade-off here between short run business interests and the wider interests of society.

> **Regulation** means applying rules to businesses and other organisations. They may be imposed by governments or by trade associations that want to maintain the reputation of the industry. Examples include caps on vehicle emissions and rules governing the way financial advice is given.

Indirect taxation

Tax incentives

Free market price signals can be modified by indirect taxes or subsidies. Excise duties can influence consumption and output. The main three UK excise duties are on tobacco, alcohol and petrol and diesel. Sales of all three incur heavy duties, making a significant contribution to government revenue.

> **Try this**
> Research current levels of excise duties on tobacco, alcohol and petrol.
> What share of their market prices is made up of tax?
> Do these taxes effectively improve health and the environment?

Paying taxes is not pleasurable. Excise duties are defended as an incentive to make better choices. However, a 'fuel duty escalator' aimed at encouraging a shift away from dependence on fossil fuels, proved deeply unpopular and was replaced by a 'fuel price stabiliser' system in 2011. Fuel is a significant cost for many businesses. Duties can have unintended consequences. One risk is that if a product is bought by the poor, a tax makes them poorer.

Think

The British Medical Journal estimates that in the two poorest socioeconomic groups, a relatively high proportion of people are addicted to tobacco. What implications does the heavy duty on tobacco have for children in poor families where both parents smoke regularly?

The UK government once estimated that 63% of hand rolled tobacco used was illegally imported. Once in the country, unofficial sales of this tobacco escaped regulation, such as age limits. The duty created potential profits for smugglers so was counterproductive in significant ways.

Grants and subsidies

Subsidies

Buyers of electric cars in Britain receive a 25% **subsidy** (up to £5,000) from the UK government. Electric cars are seen as cleaner and so to be encouraged. Renewable energy developments are given subsidies and other financial incentives, in the hope of reducing dependence on fossil and imported fuels. Energy efficiency is encouraged by incentives to insulate homes and to replace old and inefficient boilers.

A **subsidy** is a payment per unit sold which effectively shifts a supply curve downwards. Usually, the price falls and quantity increases, as shown below.

Figure 18.1: A subsidy

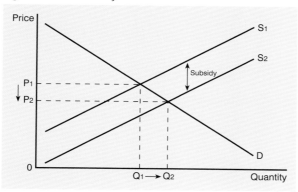

Subsidies are far more popular than taxation but they have an opportunity cost – other public spending or lower taxes. Subsidies on rice in India, intended to help the poor, often go astray in corrupt or unintended ways. The Common Agricultural Policy directs 40% of all EU spending as subsidies to the farming community; this is one reason for the EU's unpopularity in some circles.

Voluntary agreements

Voluntary standards

In 2013 a 'traffic light' system of food labelling was agreed voluntarily by major UK supermarkets. Particularly unhealthy levels of sugar, fat and salt are highlighted in red in this system. Also in 2013, the major UK banks reached a voluntary agreement on provision of basic bank accounts. Oliver Letwin, a conservative minister in the UK government since 2010, gave four reasons for emphasising a non-regulatory (voluntary) approach: "effectiveness, cost-effectiveness, less rigid imposition on individuals and reduced burden on business."

In its 4th January 2015 edition, *The Observer* reported that the voluntary standards of care for laser eye surgery, covered in 'Good Medical Practice' from the General Medical Council, "are not always being followed by high street providers." The results of this have sometimes been troubling. Firms negotiating voluntary agreements might find ways to soften the impact on their business, even if that comes at the expense of consumers or society. Some agreements are worded loosely, potentially allowing firms to go against the intended spirit, without risking any formal penalty. Executives can put the interests of their shareholders ahead of wider considerations.

> **Think**
> Would you support government regulation of procedures such as laser eye surgery or cosmetic surgery?

When government interventions fail – some examples

Potential failures

● *Administration costs may be very high.* The EU issues businesses with permits for CO_2 pollution, based on past levels. If they wish to produce and pollute more, they must buy permits from other firms. If they find cleaner ways to operate, they can sell their spare permit capacity. This gives firms incentives to find cleaner ways of working. The proposed limit (or cap) on CO_2 for 2020 is 21% lower than the starting cap in 2005; overall pollution (from 11,000 factories and power stations) is falling towards that target. This is a complex system, expensive to run and possibly open to abuse, but it represents an attempt to harness market forces with more flexibility than some alternative routes to CO_2 reduction.

● *There may be unintended consequences* – as when tobacco taxes make people on low incomes even poorer.

● *Governments may lack relevant and crucial information.* They may not know what the true cost of intervention is, or the value of the total benefit that might result. Decisions may be based on political attitudes rather than hard evidence.

● *Price signals may be distorted* – subsidies may make a product look cheaper than it really is, encouraging people to buy more of the product than they would if the price reflected the true cost of production.

> **Show your understanding**
> Using the information above and the table below, think of two specific examples of government failure, explain the issues and show why there may be a problem.

Government intervention

Action	Main Advantages	Main disadvantages	Examples
Public sector provision	Ability to choose exactly what is done.	Can be inefficient with no need for profits.	State schools. NHS. Police. Armed forces.
Legislation – bans	Clear cut – no nonsense.	Can create potential criminal profits. Need enforcement.	Rare bird eggs. Some drugs. Weapons of mass destruction.
Legislation – regulation	Can focus on cutting external costs.	Costs of implementation and enforcement.	Limits on smoking. Road traffic regulations.
Indirect taxation	Deters some buyers. Raises revenue for government.	Ineffective if price has little impact on demand. Can hit poor people hard.	Excise duties on alcohol, tobacco, oil, gambling, air travel.
Grants & Subsidies	Create incentives.	Can be costly.	Eco-friendly energy. Home insulation.
Voluntary agreements	Keeps producers onside.	Can be ineffective or/and evaded.	Food labelling.
Tradable permits	Set limits on external costs. Incentives for firms.	Expensive/difficult implementation.	EU scheme on CO_2 emissions.

Exam style question

Transport for London (TfL)

Early 21st century London road journey statistics:

Average speed of vehicles on slowest 10% of London roads: peak times	6 mph (c.9 kph)
Average speed of vehicles on slowest 10% of London roads: off-peak	9 mph (c.15 kph)
Share of average journey time spent stationary	30%

Crossrail

The TfL Crossrail project involves spending £15bn for a railway line between East and West London. It includes new tunnels under central London. TfL identifies the objectives as to:

- support development of London as a world city and financial centre;
- support economic growth and regeneration;
- improve rail access into and within London.

Regeneration

Travelling will become easier and quicker. Crowding on London's transport network will be reduced. There are substantial economic benefits for London, the southeast and the UK. Claims include adding £20 billion p.a. to the UK GDP; 20,000 people switching from cars to public transport; and regeneration of rundown areas of East London.

There is some opposition to Crossrail. Compulsory purchase orders have given 3 months notice to vacate premises. Many East Londoners suggest that travellers will simply cross their area without stopping, bringing no regeneration. No new trains will run before 2020, after 10 years of diversions, delays, noise and dust. Many of the costs and even more of the benefits of this project are externalities. Some of the projected benefits are not guaranteed. Those who suffer external costs are not all guaranteed compensation or benefits to offset their costs.

Congestion charging

London Congestion Charge Zone

The standard charge for entering the zone rose to £11.50 per day in 2014. Some greener vehicles are exempted from the charge. Non-payment brings a penalty of between £65 and £195. TfL claim that the number of chargeable vehicles entering the zone has been reduced by 30%. Traffic moves more freely, with fewer delays. Accident casualties and pollution have both been reduced. All money raised by the charge is reinvested in the wider transport network. TfL estimates that the overall effect on business has been neutral.

There have been winners and losers from the congestion charge. The John Lewis Partnership announced that in the first six months of the charge's operation, sales at their Oxford Street store fell by 7.3%; sales at stores in Greater London but outside the Congestion Charge Zone rose by 1.7%. Roads and parking places just outside the zone have become more congested. In 2013/14 £150m was paid in charges and there were £45m of penalties. *The Daily Telegraph* said "Everyone who lives in the capital knows that the congestion charge fails to control congestion but acts as one more tax" (13 December 2014).

Questions

1. What is meant by 'external costs'? *(2 marks)*
2. Explain two external costs of Crossrail *(4 marks)*
3. Explain two external benefits from the Congestion Charge. *(4 marks)*
4. Examine reasons why Crossrail is unlikely to have been undertaken as a private sector business. *(8 marks)*
5. Evaluate the economic case for Crossrail and for the Congestion Charge. *(12 marks)*

Chapter 19

Calculating revenue and costs

TerraCycle

TerraCycle is a recycling and upcycling business which aims to find waste and turn it into something useful, for a profit. Founder Tom Szaky moved from Hungary to the USA and was struck by the mountains of material thrown out in rich communities. TerraCycle's first activity was collecting organic waste and feeding it to worms, then selling the resulting fertiliser in recycled plastic bottles, as plant food.

Not all activities have been profitable. A bag called the 'reTote', made from used plastic bags, was sold to a distributor for a few dollars each though the costs were more than $10 per unit. Despite this, the company has grown in 13 years, to have revenue of $20m p.a. and 115 employees. It operates in several countries.

Much of the collection of waste materials is now done by volunteers organised in 'brigades'. The volunteers get nothing tangible for themselves but are rewarded by donations to charity and "a good feeling". TerraCycle make few products themselves. They collect the waste and design products and processes. Others are then licensed to make, market and sell the products. An unnamed British company is in talks to buy 20% of the business for around $20m.

Discussion points

1. Identify costs likely to have contributed to the 'reTote' average of more than $10 per unit.

2. Suggest possible costs to TerraCycle of working with their volunteer waste collection 'brigades'.

3. Why might a company be prepared to pay $20m for 20% of TerraCycle?

4. Suggest two ways in which TerraCycle's current owners could use the $20m.

Adding value

Put simply, businesses operate by taking *inputs*, changing them in ways that *add value*, and producing *outputs*.

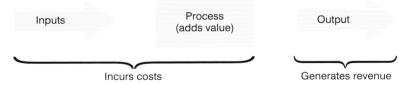

Outputs (which can be measured by quantity) are sold in order to generate sales revenue (cash). Sales revenue is money made by the business when selling goods or services. The process of producing outputs incurs costs for the business. These costs of production must be paid for. We can classify costs, placing them in different groups.

Sales volume

> The total physical quantity of products sold is the **sales volume**.
>
> The total of incoming payments for products sold is the **sales revenue** (price x quantity sold).

Classifying costs

Capital spending

Start-up costs

These are initial costs faced when a business is set up. They only need to be paid once. They include:

- payments for services such as business advice and market research.
- fixtures and fittings.
- tools, machines and specialist equipment needed to create the product.

These costs are usually paid before the business starts trading, so finance is needed to cover them until enough revenue is earned to pay them off.

Capital spending

In the case study above, Terracycle's start-up costs included premises for the worms and waste products and vehicles to transport waste and fertiliser.

Businesses can also incur significant one-off costs when making large changes or additions to operations. For example, starting reTote production required new machinery and staff training.

TerraCycle now needs space for 115 people to work and facilities for receiving and processing different types of waste. This involved a large financial outlay which had to be paid for somehow.

Investment

Start-up and capital costs include many items that would be classified as investment. When a business buys premises and equipment that will last and make it possible to produce over a period of years, they are investing now in order to have sales revenue and profit in the future. Often, we regard spending on training or research into possible new products as investment too. Training makes employees more efficient and productive.

Start-up costs are incurred in setting up a business organisation.

Capital spending occurs when a business invests in premises or equipment or something of long term benefit to the business.

Investment involves spending now which generates income in the future. Examples include buying capital equipment or spending on research or training.

Fixed, variable and total costs

So far we have discussed production costs in general. Sometimes these are called **running costs** or **operating costs**, because they keep the business running – the business has to pay for them so long as it is active. They fall into two categories: *fixed costs* and *variable costs*. Total costs include both. (Many things in the economy and in business have several names.)

Fixed costs

Fixed costs are not directly affected by how much the business produces. For example, insurance, utility bills and rent or mortgage payments have to be paid each month regardless of how much has been produced. These costs are not 'fixed' for ever. For example, it is common for rents and utility charges to increase with inflation. The key issue here is that the level of fixed costs is *not linked to the level of output*. A rising level of output will not immediately affect fixed costs.

If a business grows significantly it is likely that fixed costs will increase, especially in the long term. This is because growth may require larger premises – so higher rent, utility and insurance costs. Additional staff may be recruited, increasing the overall cost of salaries. However, one extra unit of output will not directly incur extra costs in any of these areas.

Variable costs

Variable costs are *directly linked to the level of output* of a business. They are the costs of resources used to produce units of output, or to deliver a service. They include raw materials, components and often the cost of labour used in the production process. If the level of output rises, total variable costs will also increase.

Labour costs can be fixed or variable. If a member of staff, e.g. an accountant, is paid a fixed salary regardless of how much work they do, their payment is a fixed cost because it doesn't change according to output. If they are paid directly according to how much they produce (for example, freelancers or employees on zero hours contracts) then the wage is a variable cost because it goes up directly when the employee works and produces more.

TerraCycle's labour costs are low when volunteers collect materials but most of the 115 employees are on fixed salaries. The variable costs include everything directly linked to sorting and processing the waste to prepare it for reuse.

> **Operating costs** or **running costs** are paid regularly by a business in the course of operating. They include fixed and variable costs and correspond to total costs.
>
> **Fixed costs** are not directly linked to the level of output of the business. They do not change when output increases or decreases. These are sometimes called *indirect costs* or *overheads*. Fixed costs include all capital spending but also some regular costs such as staff salaries.
>
> **Variable costs** are directly linked to the level of output of the business. They change as output increases or decreases. These are sometimes called *direct costs*. They include materials and the cost of paying any employees paid solely according their contribution to actual production.

Example

In Chapter 12 you met Stephanie, a hairdresser. When Stephanie set up her salon she had to pay a number of start-up costs: she had to buy chairs, dryers, other specialist equipment, towels and a cash till, for example.

Now that Stephanie is running her business she has to pay some fixed monthly costs: she has rent, public liability insurance and a water bill, for example. These are all fixed costs because they have to be paid whether the salon sees one client or a hundred clients. In fact, if she had no customers at all, she would still have to pay these fixed costs.

Each time a customer is served this incurs some additional costs. She has to pay for consumables such as shampoos, sprays and colourants; also to launder the towels used during hair washing. These are variable costs because the more clients the salon has, the more she will have to pay for consumables and laundry.

Show your understanding

Calculating

Stephanie's fixed costs each year amount to £30,000 for rent and £8,000 for utilities (power and water). Consumables cost £10,000 and services such as accountancy and insurance cost another £5,000. She pays herself £25,000 a year and spends £20,000 paying her regular staff for a fixed number of hours each week (she doesn't approve of zero hours contracts). Business rates take a further £10,000 and interest and repayment to the bank will be £10,000. Usually she needs to pay a further £82,000 for employees who come in on busy days and for the cleaner.

Work out Stephanie's total fixed costs and total variable costs.

Average and total costs

Once a business is operating, start-up costs should be a thing of the past; though interest and repayments might still be due on any borrowed money. Capital equipment will gradually become less useful (this is called **depreciation**) and some items will need replacing or updating from time to time. Any spending on such things will be included in total costs. These are the sum of all the costs incurred in a time period – often a year. There will be fixed costs even with no output. As output increases, variable costs and so total costs will increase.

> **Depreciation** is the loss in value of capital equipment over time, often due to wear and tear or technology becoming dated.

Total variable costs

All of the increase in total cost, once output is more than zero, will be **variable costs**, so the red line in Figure 19.2 shows that fixed costs don't change with output. The total variable cost line (TVC) looks curvy because putting in extra inputs will not always have the same effect on output.

Figure 19.1: Total costs

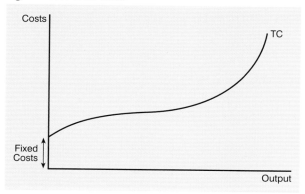

Back in Stephanie's hairdressing business, having a second and third person working at any time is useful and three people can probably handle more than 3 times the work of 1. With more people, the salon will get crowded. Eventually extra people will be waiting for seats and staff will get in each other's way, so each extra employee will get less work done.

Figure 19.2: The make-up of total costs

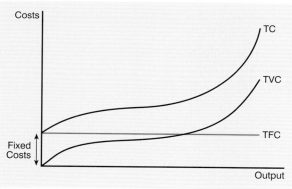

Law of diminishing returns

Average variable costs

Once extra variable inputs add less to output, it will take more time and so cost more to increase output. The cost of extra units will rise. Economists call this the **law of diminishing returns**. The result of this is that when we plot **average variable cost**, the cost per unit might fall at first but will eventually rise. We expect average total cost and average variable costs to slope down then up, as shown in Figure 19.3, page 102.

> If one or more factors of production is fixed, adding more and more of a variable factor will eventually add less to output. This is the **law of diminishing returns**.
>
> **Average variable costs** are the total of variable costs divided by output.

Average variable, fixed and total cost

Average total costs tend to fall as output increases because better use is being made of the fixed factors of production – the premises and the equipment. So as Stephanie gets more customers, average costs will fall. At the bottom of the curve, costs will be minimised because she will be fully booked all the time. In practice, output won't increase much beyond that because Stephanie will either make the customers wait or put the price up. (See page 102.)

Average, fixed and variable costs

Notice in Figure 19.3, as output increases, average fixed costs will fall as they are spread across more customers. Average variable costs would rise as more staff have to be brought in; they might, for example, want a pay rise.

> **Show your understanding**
> Calculate average total, fixed and variable cost for each appointment if Stephanie gets 6,000 appointments per year.

Figure 19.3: Average, fixed, variable and total costs

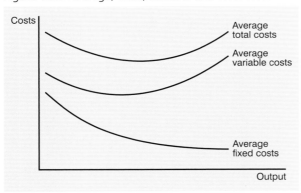

Percentages

The balance between fixed and variable costs depends on the type of business. A small hydroelectric system (generating electricity) might have a fixed start-up cost of £250m (e.g. land, dam, turbines) and operating costs of £10m p.a. Stephanie might have fixed costs of £100,000 and variable costs each year of the same amount. Comparisons would be difficult because the hairdressing salon is on a much smaller scale.

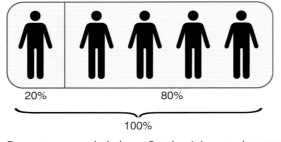

Calculating percentages

Percentages can help here. Stephanie's annual operating costs are 100% of her fixed costs (£100k ÷ £100k x 100). The equivalent for the hydroelectric system would be £10m ÷ £250m x 100 = 0.04 x 100 = 4%. The percentage quickly shows the contrast between a business with a relatively low share of fixed costs and a business where fixed costs are by far the greatest expense.

> **Calculating percentages**
> Take the relevant figure (£10m for the hydroelectric system example).
>
> Checking units are the same; divide it by the relevant total (£250m in the same example).
>
> Multiply the result by 100.
>
> Calculator method: Input 1st value ÷ 2nd value x 100. Don't press % but write % after answer.
>
> *If your result looks crazy, repeat the process as errors are easily made.*

Figure 19.4 shows what to do using random numbers.

Figure 19.4: Calculating percentages

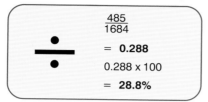

$$\frac{485}{1684}$$

$$= 0.288$$

$$0.288 \times 100$$

$$= 28.8\%$$

Percentage changes

Percentages and percentage changes are useful in studying the performance of any business. Percentage changes in sales volume, sales revenue and costs are often the quickest way to see how a business is doing. Apple announced record figures for the last quarter of 2014. Sales revenue had risen to $74.6bn from $57.6bn a year earlier. 74.5 million iPhones were sold (though Samsung led on sales volume with 78 million sales). Sales in China rose 70%. Profits were up to $18bn from $13.1bn a year earlier

Try this

Calculate the percentage changes in Apple's sales revenue and profit from the data shown above. How impressive are these figures?

Samsung's sales volume was bigger; do you think their revenue will have been greater too?

⚠ WATCH OUT!

When you are asked to make calculations in an exam, this is often followed by a question about interpreting or commenting on the data you have calculated.

Exam style question

Peter Huan

Peter is a self-employed taxi driver in Kuala Lumpur (Malaysia).

To buy and equip his taxi he used savings and borrowed from Kiva (an online crowdfunding organisation that supports small-scale business start-ups and expansion). On average he works for ten hours per day, mainly splitting those hours between mornings and evenings, to work when demand is higher. His typical monthly costs are shown in the table. Some of these are fixed costs and others depend on how much business he does.

Monthly cost	$
Loan repayment	250
Petrol	400
Insurance	80
Advertising	30
Telephone charges	40

Questions

1. What is meant by fixed costs? *(2 marks)*

2. Give an example of a variable cost from the table and explain why it is variable. *(4 marks)*

3. Peter's revenue in October was $1,700. Calculate his total cost and his profit for the month. *(4 marks)*

4. Kiva supporters receive no interest on loans they make, but are normally repaid. Discuss the value of Kiva to borrowers and to lenders. *(8 marks)*

5. Peter had 200 customers in October. Assess two ways in which he could reduce his average cost, using some calculation to support your suggestions. *(12 marks)*

Chapter 20

Exploring the links between costs, revenue and profit

Selling memory

Kelvin has become a part-time eBay trader, slowly building up his business. He sold a few unwanted items from home and then his CDs (which he first stored electronically). Now he specialises in novelty usb memory sticks, in moulded plastic shapes such as cartoon characters or guitars. He started selling these using the eBay 'buy it now' system with a fixed

price, generally around £6. Now he uses a combined approach, auctioning with no reserve price but also including a 'buy it now' option.

He buys in bulk from Hong Kong at an average total cost around £3.50 (excluding onward postage for which he adds a charge). Sometimes his auctioned items sell at low prices, but he doesn't see this as a problem. He finds that low initial bids for auctioned items attract buyers to his sale. Many of these buyers are either impatient or fear not winning at auction. As a result, he sells more 'buy it now' items at £6 than he did when not offering the auction option. This business takes up an hour or two most evenings and he makes daily trips to the post office. Kelvin has reached the point where he is thinking about giving up his main job, adding more products, and becoming a full-time trader.

Discussion points

1. What risks are involved in Kelvin's business?

2. Should he count his own time as a cost?

3. Why might he be tempted to become a full-time trader?

In Chapter 2 (page 6) you looked at profit as a business objective. Now we examine the relationship between **sales revenue**, costs and **profit**. Remember the basic connections:

PROFIT = SALES REVENUE – COST

SALES REVENUE = (SALES VOLUME x SELLING PRICE)

Loss

If costs are greater than sales revenue, then the business is making a **loss** and important decision are needed in order to turn it around. First and foremost will be the question of how to increase sales revenue.

Profit is the money remaining from sales revenue after all costs have been paid. It is the entrepreneur's reward for investing their personal resources (time, enterprise, assets) in a business and taking risks.

Sales revenue is money earned by selling goods and services. It is calculated by multiplying the sales volume by the unit selling price.

Sales volume refers to the number of goods or services sold by a business in a period of time.

Selling price is the amount charged to a customer for the purchase of a good or service.

A business makes a **loss** when revenue earned is less than total costs.

Analysing costs, revenue and profit

Living with his parents allows Kelvin to see everything he gets above £3.50 for a memory stick as profit. If he went full-time he would have to rent premises, perhaps on a local business park. His research suggests that he would then have fixed costs of around £500 per week. Using the unit cost and price shown above (£3.50 AVC and price £6) is a simplification because his range of products would increase, but it is a useful simplification. On a typical sale, the £2.50 left after paying the variable cost would be a contribution towards either meeting fixed costs or to profit.

Contribution

> **Contribution** is the amount each sale raises towards fixed costs or profit.
>
> Mathematically, **contribution** = selling price – variable costs. In this case £6 - £.3.50 = £2.50

We can see that if he goes full-time, he would need to sell 200 memory sticks per week just to cover his fixed costs (as 200 x £2.50 = £500). If he took a week off and sold nothing, he would lose £500 that week. Once sales go above 200 per week, he would make profits. This means that 200 sales per week would be his break-even point. His position would be as shown below:

Sales	Costs and Revenue	Outcome
Zero	Fixed costs only, Revenue zero	Loss (£500)
Below breakeven (1-199)	Fixed costs + variable costs > Revenue	Smaller loss
Breakeven (200)	Fixed costs + variable costs = Revenue	No loss, no profit
Above breakeven >200	Fixed costs + variable costs < Revenue	Profits made

Kelvin also has regular auction sales at variable prices. When an auctioned memory stick sells at above £3.50, it makes a contribution – but sometimes a small one. Only on sales at below £3.50 does he make a loss.

Break-even point

Businesses normally have fixed costs and variable costs. A business producing zero units of output will still have to pay fixed costs but will have no sales revenue. It will therefore be making a loss with costs greater than revenue (which is zero). As units are produced these will contribute towards paying the fixed costs, and eventually the total revenue will exactly cover the costs. The point at which costs are equal to revenue is called the **break-even point** or the break-even level of sales. It is very useful to know what this is in a business, to make judgements about how likely it is to be profitable. Assembling and using the data for this is called break-even analysis. At the break-even point:

TOTAL FIXED COSTS + TOTAL VARIABLE COSTS = TOTAL SALES REVENUE

Identifying the break-even revenue

We can calculate the number of contributions needed to pay off the fixed costs by using either one of these formulae:

Covering fixed costs

$$\frac{\textbf{FIXED COSTS}}{\textbf{CONTRIBUTION}} \quad or \quad \frac{\textbf{FIXED COSTS}}{\textbf{(SP - AVC)}}$$

(SP above is selling price, AVC is average variable cost)

 **WATCH OUT!**

Although these calculations use money values, the result they give is a quantity of output (needed to raise break-even revenue).

Break-even analysis

> **Break-even point** is the volume of sales at which a business breaks even, so total revenue matches total costs exactly.
>
> **Break-even analysis** is the calculation and interpretation of information about the break-even sales level.

> **Try this**
> A market trader pays £72 per day for a stall where he sells watches for £8. They cost him £5 each. Ignoring other costs, calculate the contribution of each watch and the break-even level of sales.

Margin of safety

Margin of safety

At any level of sales above the BE point, a business is profitable. There is a number of units by which sales volume can fall before reaching the BE point, known as the **margin of safety**. The larger the margin of safety, the greater a fall in sales the business can absorb before making a loss. The business shown below has sales of 2,200, a BE point at 1,000 units and so a margin of safety of 2,200 − 1,000 = 1,200 units

Figure 20.1: Break-even chart for a profitable business

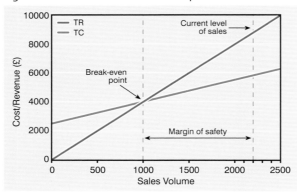

> **Margin of safety** = the volume by which sales are above the break-even point.
>
> Calculated as expected sales (or actual sales) − break-even sales level.

The purpose of break-even analysis

Using break-even

Break-even analysis (or BE analysis) can be used for a number of different purposes:

● **To inform pricing decisions**

A business may calculate the break-even level of sales at a range of different prices as a way of helping to decide how much to charge for a product or service. It will want to be confident that predicted sales volumes will allow the business to make enough profit, bearing in mind potential demand.

● **To predict profit**

If a business is in a competitive situation it may have to accept the market price, with no real choice about the price charged. It may, therefore, use BE analysis as a tool to predict how much profit can be made at different volumes of sales.

● **To seek finance**

Investors and lenders will only commit money to a business idea if they are confident that it will be profitable. BE analysis can form part of a business plan. This is a document used to promote a business idea to potential investors or lenders.

● To conduct 'what-if' analysis

Modelling the impact of change

Businesses may want to 'model' the impact of changes, such as changing price or to forecast the impact of possible changes in demand, or in fixed or variable costs. BE analysis allows such changes to be included in a BE calculation so that new BE levels can be identified. If demand (or total sales) is forecast to change, BE analysis can focus on the margin of safety and whether the business is likely to remain profitable.

Limitations of break-even analysis

BE analysis assumes that fixed and variable costs are known. Especially during business planning, an entrepreneur may have to make a 'best guess' at costs. Hence, the quality of BE analysis will depend on the accuracy of the assumptions made.

Assumptions matter

Estimates made using market research will be based on evidence from before pricing decisions are made. In a dynamic economy there are many variables that could change during the time lag between research and final decisions. For example, consumer tastes and incomes, resource costs and competitor innovations can change the situation, either individually or in some combination. Alertness and readiness to modify assumptions can help, but it can become necessary to go back to square one.

Where prices fluctuate frequently or different prices are charged for the same product, BE analysis needs simplifying assumptions about pricing as well as about costs. It is dangerously easy to make optimistic assumptions in this situation.

Will the product sell?

BE analysis identifies total revenue and profit at different sales volumes. However, it doesn't guarantee that a business will generate sufficient demand to sell at this level. Besides forecasting costs, the business needs to be able to judge accurately the likely demand for the product, if it is to calculate useful BE data. BE analysis can highlight the need to market the product more effectively in order to reach the sales volume needed to cover costs.

Exam style question

Paellapile

Sian Lang worked as a chef in a pub/restaurant before starting her own catering service. This has expanded to cover weddings, company gatherings and public events. Friends have advised her that her paellas would sell well at The Glastonbury Festival.

Research into this proved it was an attractive opportunity but not an easy one. Over 170,000 people are at Worthy Farm over the long festival weekend. Few of them have the facilities or the inclination to prepare their own food. The potential market is enormous by Sian's standards. On the other hand, there are more than 250 food stalls on site and both the costs and the conditions laid down are demanding. Her informed estimate was that setting up a decent stall (if her application succeeded), with the festival licence plus fitting out and staffing it, would cost her £10,000. The fact that many traders return year after year demonstrated that making a profit must still be possible.

Her variable costs (from food to disposable plates) would be slightly higher for her chicken and seafood paella than for the vegetarian version, which seemed just as popular elsewhere, but the average across the two would be £3 per portion. Well presented, the paella sells elsewhere for £7.

Questions

1. What is meant by variable costs? *(2 marks)*
2. Calculate Sian's breakeven output if she takes a festival stall. Show your working. *(4 marks)*
3. Explain why Sian decided to treat staffing as a fixed cost in this situation. *(4 marks)*
4. Discuss reasons why Sian's break-even estimate could prove to be wrong. *(8 marks)*
5. Assess the role of a margin of safety in this situation. *(12 marks)*

Chapter 21

Exploring profit and loss

The Grebe Hotel

Anna and Michael grew tired of their busy lives as a social worker and a hospital administrator. Commuting to work around suburban London ate into their time. Both were sociable people and Michael was an enthusiastic amateur chef. They decided that running a small hotel or guesthouse business together would offer them a better lifestyle. Visiting Blackpool, they were pleasantly surprised at how cheap hotels were, and they settled on the 22 bedroom Grebe Hotel which was on the seafront to the North of the town centre. The freehold price was only £375,000 whereas their house in the South of England sold for more than £500,000.

In Blackpool they found that their personal spending fell, thanks to savings on travel and lunches; also the cost of living was lower there. However, they found that tourism in Blackpool was intensely competitive (with fewer traditional seaside holidays being taken) and running the hotel was tiring. At the bottom of the market, price competition kept margins wafer thin, despite various short cuts people took to cut costs.

They chose to focus on quality, with spotless cleanliness, big breakfasts and smart, cheerful service. They even used savings to give attractive makeovers to some 'themed' rooms. When they bought their hotel, they had been shown accounts with turnover above £100,000 per year. Progress was slow and they took just £70,000 in their second year. £34,000 of that was taken up by variable costs such as food, laundry and the two part-time employees who cleaned and helped.

Discussion points

1. Should Anna and Michael include their working time as a variable cost?

2. What is the opportunity cost of tying up the money from their house sale in the business?

3. Why was a clean and tidy hotel in Blackpool cheaper than their former house?

Profit as an incentive

Profit matters

The Grebe Hotel experience shows that making money out of a business is seldom easy. Had they kept their former jobs, they could have earned more and worked fewer hours. However, we saw in Chapter 2 that people have a variety of business objectives. Even where objectives centre on lifestyle, ethics or safeguarding the planet, rather than profit maximisation, people need to eat. Running at a loss is not sustainable.

The long-term switch in emphasis to overseas holidays has left a surplus of accommodation in resorts such as Blackpool and the town now has low incomes and high unemployment. Many hoteliers have sold up and left; they have decided to **exit** the market. Others wish they could sell up but feel trapped by mortgage debt and falling hotel prices. There are success stories with good USPs, but market signals suggest this is not an industry with high profits. Further evidence for this comes from the number of hotels now converted to alternative uses such as care homes for the elderly.

Exit

Resources tend to move away (exit) from unprofitable industries. Hotel buildings have alternative uses. Not all resources are easily transferable, though. A switch to more reliance on oil and gas meant demand for coal fell a generation ago. Much equipment was simply abandoned. Miners struggled to find work; new jobs were often in distant locations or required skills they did not have.

Figure 21.1: Movement of resources

Entry

Example

Penny Scott saved a struggling service by opening a coffee shop in a side room at her local public library. Local government spending cuts threatened the library. Coffee shops are doing well and the library coffee shop was quickly profitable. The latest development is a shared staffing deal which has made it possible to increase the library opening hours. More coffee shops have entered the market because it is a profitable business. Coupling Penny's coffee shop with the library has been a success.

Barriers to entry

Resources move into attractive and profitable industries – a process known as **entry**. But obstacles often deter new entrants. These are called **barriers to entry**. Some industries require large scale capital investment which a small business would struggle to finance. Think of commercial aircraft manufacture, for example. It would take £billions to set up a new plane maker. Start-up costs would be hard to recover; such **sunk costs** would mean a crippling loss if the business failed.

Sometimes there are legal barriers imposed by governments. A one car taxi business would be a relatively easy business start-up, except that taxis need licences and many authorities issue only a set number of these. Existing firms can deliberately deter new rivals, for example by spending heavily on marketing, signing exclusive deals with retail outlets or controlling the supply of materials. Profits stay high in some industries because barriers to entry protect existing firms and give them market power. There is suspicion that the six dominant electricity and gas retailers have exploited market power. Resources can't always be shifted as simply as basic theory suggest.

> **Barriers to entry** are obstacles to new entrants which affect some industries, particularly where competing businesses are very large.
>
> Heavy start-up costs which cannot be recovered are **sunk costs**. They increase the risks of entry, acting as a deterrent or barrier.
>
> Market **entry** refers to businesses that set up in, or move into, a new market. **Exit** occurs if they cannot make a profit and can find no way of competing effectively.

Calculating profit

Keeping track of the finances is essential for assessing business performance, planning for the future and for tax purposes. An important part of company accounts is the '**statement of comprehensive income**', which in small businesses is still sometimes referred to as the profit and loss account.

WATCH OUT!

Unfortunately, economists and accountants often use different words for the same thing. Sometimes there is also common sense wording which is different again. The way accounts are recorded has changed. Older textbooks and some websites are not up to date. Add the existence of alternative names for some items and there is potential for confusion.

Statement of comprehensive income

The first important figure is the amount of money coming into the business. This is the **sales revenue** or the **turnover**. Both of these terms are widely understood. But to find out about profit, we need information on costs. **Variable costs** are the most immediate outlay linked to providing a good or service. Accountants often call this the **cost of goods sold** (**COGS**). At Grebe Hotel variable costs were £34,000 for Year 2.

When we subtract variable costs from revenue, we get **gross profit** – our first measure of how a business is doing. This is still only a weak indication of profitability because there are more costs to come. A business that can't make a gross profit must be losing money and should think seriously about whether to carry on.

Then the **fixed costs** or **overheads** must be taken into account. Clear examples of fixed costs are the IT system and other equipment. At Grebe Hotel, rooms had to be kept warm in case unexpected guests arrived; heating and other fixed costs came to £8,000. It is normal for owners who work in a business to pay themselves a fixed salary, in this case £25,000.

Once fixed costs are deducted from gross profit, we have **operating profit**. This is a better measure of business performance. Operating profit figures are frequently quoted in company reports and in the press. However, this is not the end of the story as there are yet more deductions.

Businesses can't keep all their profits because they have tax liabilities. Even those multinationals who shuffle their accounting to avoid heavy tax generally pay something, somewhere. The Grebe Hotel didn't have to pay profits tax but it did have to pay business tax to the local authority.

Both large and small businesses use loans. The interest on these loans is another cost. When we deduct tax and interest from operating profit, we finally arrive at **profit for the year**, also known as **net profit**. Owners can choose whether to plough profits back into fresh investment or to take this money as their own. Accounts looks backwards rather than forwards because it is only possible to total everything up at the end of the trading period.

Figure 21.2: The Grebe Hotel's Year 2 figures – a simplified account

Calculating profit and loss

Revenue, costs and profit	Figures	Meaning
Revenue	£70,000	
COGS	£34,000	Variable costs
Gross profit	£36,000	Revenue – variable costs
Overheads	£33,000	Fixed costs including salaries
Operating profit	£3,000	Gross profit – fixed costs
Tax and interest	£4,000	Business rates + mortgage interest
Net profit	-£1,000	

Sales revenue — minus variable costs — = gross profit — minus fixed costs — = operating profit — minus tax and interest — = profit for the year

Turnover and **sales revenue** are names for the sum of payments received, normally for a year.

The **statement of comprehensive income**, also called the **profit and loss account**, starts with a figure for sales revenue and deducts each different group of costs to arrive at measures of profit.

Variable costs, also known as **cost of goods sold** (**COGS**) are the costs of inputs to the production process, e.g. labour, components, raw materials. This excludes overheads and will vary directly with the amount produced.

Net profit

> **Gross profit** means sales revenue less the immediate variable costs of producing the goods sold.
>
> **Fixed costs** or **overheads** are the costs that stay the same regardless of how much is produced.
>
> **Profit for the year** or **net profit** is what remains from sales revenue after the deduction of all operating costs, including overheads, tax and interest payable. If a loss has been made figures are shown in brackets. Net profit is a revealing measure of performance which can be used to make comparisons over a number of years.

Show your understanding
How might Anna and Michael try to reduce their losses and generate some net profit? Think of and explain three possibilities.

Using ratios to measure profitability

Profit margins

Anna and Michael would be content, and relieved, if their hotel produced just enough profit to allow them to save something for the future. £50,000 would be plenty for them. McDonalds made a profit for the year of $1.07 billion in 2014, which disappointed them as it represented a 30% fall on 2013. Just comparing profit totals gives limited information. A global fast food chain expects more than one smallish hotel. Using ratios allows us to make more useful comparisons, for example on how effective businesses are at turning revenue into profit. Profit margins are ratios expressed as percentages.

Gross profit margin is gross profit as a percentage of sales revenue. Comparisons over time tell us how well the business is using its inputs.

$$\text{Gross profit margin} \quad = \quad \frac{\text{Gross profit x 100}}{\text{Sales revenue}}$$

Operating profit margin is operating profit as a percentage of sales revenue. It gives information about how efficiently the business is using all of its resources.

$$\text{Operating profit margin} \quad = \quad \frac{\text{Operating profit x 100}}{\text{Sales revenue}}$$

At the risk of boring you, **net profit margin** uses the same method. It is a measure of financial performance and indicates how shareholders may be rewarded.

$$\text{Net profit margin} \quad = \quad \frac{\text{Net profit x 100}}{\text{Sales revenue}}$$

We looked at percentage calculation in Chapter 19 (pages 102-3) on revenue and costs. Revising this may help with calculations. An important priority here is to pick the right profit figure to work with in each case.

Interpreting the figures

There can be a trade-off which influences these margins so bigger is not always better. Supermarkets, for example, operate with relatively small margins as they rely on low prices to attract a large number of customers. For example, an operating profit of 3% on cans of beans is OK when large supermarket branches sell thousands of cans. A small shop in a village would sell far less and 3% on a dozen cans would only make a tiny contribution to profitability.

Interpreting accounts

We have to be careful to compare like with like. Interpreting the figures and working out what has happened to a specific business requires us to compare the accounts with those for earlier years. If we are comparing several businesses, they must be operating in the same markets, with similar products. We might look at

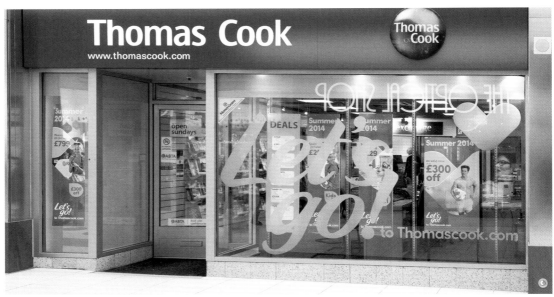

Comparing the profits of a travel agent with those of a car manufacturer would not be meaningful.

profit margins for a number of car manufacturers or several different travel agents. Comparing the profits of a travel agent with those of a car manufacturer would not be meaningful.

Calculating profit margins

> **Try this**
>
> Using the data in Figure 21.2, calculate the Grebe Hotel's year 2 gross, operating and net profit margins and comment on each. Primark reported operating profit of £662m in the year to November 2014, and sales revenue of £4.95bn. With so many noughts, a rough guideline helps avoid errors. £662m is roughly two thirds of a billion; these profits were above a tenth (10%) of £4.3bn but below 20%. Try to calculate a more accurate operating profit margin.
>
> Why might this be a smaller operating profit margin than a small antique shop requires?

Using accounts

Budding entrepreneurs who need to attract bank finance or to impress individual investors must produce estimated statements of comprehensive income. Established businesses need to look back at the accounts from the past for a whole range of reasons:

● to identify trends over time. These can be very revealing.

● to raise finance, as proof of past performance is an indicator of the risk in lending. A bank will want to study all the accounts carefully.

● to analyse the success of the business in meeting its profit objectives.

● to compare with the record of similar businesses in the industry, in order to judge efficiency.

● to set objectives for the future.

Improving profits

Anna and Michael could see from their year 2 profit and loss accounts that they would need to change something. Getting better known was creating some repeat visits but that was not enough. In year 3 they planned to use 'flash sales' offering cheap rooms to their database of customers, which could make a contribution. Apart from this, they wanted to focus on adding value and developing a brand image rather than to be drawn into fierce price competition. Cutting costs would help if possible, but cuts which reduced the quality of guest experience would be dangerous. The first few years of a new business are frequently tough and rapid failure is all too common. In general, these are the possibilities:

Improving profits

- *Reducing COGS* can mean using the available labour more efficiently, or cutting the cost of inputs, perhaps by finding cheaper suppliers.

- *Reducing overheads* can be achieved in large firms if they can do administrative tasks more efficiently or can find cheaper premises or suppliers (e.g. for insurance). In extreme circumstances, salaries may be reduced. This is common in recessions.

- Increasing sales revenue by *raising prices*, but only if the market is growing, or the price rise will not put people off. If in fact there is a cheaper competing substitute for the product, this will not work.

- *Increasing marketing expenditure* if extra advertising (for example) will add less to costs than it does to revenue.

- *Cutting prices* can increase sales revenue if it means selling to a wider market. Some businesses can move from a small niche market to a mass market in this way. But the business would have to look carefully at the increase in COGS as a result of increasing output. Trying out different possibilities using breakeven might help to analyse the likely outcomes.

Try this

Now go back to your comments when responding to the questions about how the Grebe Hotel could increase profits, Show your understanding, page 111. Do you want to improve your answer?

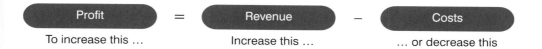

Profit	=	Revenue	−	Costs
To increase this …		Increase this …		… or decrease this

Exam style question

Intercontinental Hotels Group (IHG)

IHG operates on several continents and with more than 4,500 hotels. Their seven main brands include Intercontinental Hotels, Holiday Inn and Crowne Plaza. Nearly all of the hotels are 'franchised', owned and operated by other people who pay for the use of IHG branding and marketing. A minority are managed by IHG for their owners. Just 7 hotels are owned by IHG. Below are some (simplified) extracts from the 2013 IHG accounts:

Item	$m
Revenue	1,903
Cost of goods sold	783
Overheads	440
Interest and tax payments	250

Questions

1. What is meant by cost of goods sold? *(2 marks)*

2. Calculate (a) gross and (b) operating profit. Show your working. *(4 marks)*

3. Explain two likely major differences in the accounts if IHG owned rather than franchised most of its hotels. *(4 marks)*

4. Discuss two reasons why profit and loss accounts are important to a business. *(8 marks)*

5. With reference to the data, assess the performance of IHG. *(12 marks)*

Chapter 22

Business survival and cash flow

A business failure

Even during his apprenticeship as a printer, Mark was very interested in design, layout and appearance, as well as in working accurately. He thought that the business he worked for produced ordinary work which could easily be transformed into eye-catching material. The rush to get things done seemed more important to the managers than the quality of the finished job. Having decided that he could do better, he started his own small printing business.

He was able to lease a disused workshop and also leased up to the minute computerised printing machinery which was far better than many established businesses had. He became popular with local small businesses surprisingly quickly. After a few months he was approached by a large machinery manufacturer, based in his home city, which sold equipment multinationally. Even a trial order of printing for them was big enough to mean working very long hours. That led to more orders, more workshop space and more equipment.

Mark had priced competitively, but knew what his costs were and included a small profit margin. His problem was that the machinery manufacturer and other large business customers were very slow to pay. His invoice terms stated that payments were due in 30 days from delivery. That meant a bank loan because his major costs were payable before or during production. Large firms just seemed to ignore the 30 day period and kept him waiting. He went to the bank for a bigger loan, but at a time when they were cutting back on business lending, and they refused. When a lease payment became due to the workshop owners, Mark could not pay. The owners used hefty locks to block access to the workshops and Mark's business died – thanks to shortage of cash, not a lack of profitability.

Discussion points
1. What advantage did slow payment of bills give to the large businesses?
2. Why might court action to enforce payment from large customers be a poor idea?
3. Why might the workshop owner have been unsympathetic towards Mark's problem?

Cash flow forecasting

Businesses incur costs and generate revenue. A key issue for many businesses is that payments, or **cash outflows**, may be needed before revenue, or **cash inflows**, are generated. Running out of available cash is a fast route to **insolvency** and business failure. In the case study at the beginning of this chapter, Mark's cash inflow should eventually have been bigger than his outflow. Unfortunately, he needed to pay out for his costs before enough revenue came in.

Cash flow

A cash flow forecast aims to predict when cash outflows and inflows will occur. This enables a business to identify times when extra finance (working capital) will be needed to maintain **liquidity** by covering any cash shortfalls – they can then seek a source of finance appropriate to the amount of money and the

Liquidity

length of time for which it is needed. Holding too much cash has an opportunity cost, often in terms of interest to be paid. Holding too little can be terminal for a business. (If you are feeling hazy about working capital, go back to Chapter 7, page 30.)

A simple cash flow forecast could look like this:

Building a cash flow forecast

Table 22.1: Cash flow forecast

	Month 1 forecast	Month 1 actual	Month 2 forecast	Month 2 actual	Month 3 forecast	Month 3 actual
1. Opening balance						
2. Receipts (cash in)						
3. Outflow (payments)						
4. (2 − 3) Net change						
5. (1 + 4) Closing balance						

The simple central idea here is that each opening balance, plus the inflow and minus the outflow in the month, will determine the next month's opening balance. Plotting actual data against forecasts gives an indication of performance and also identifies any recurring issues. There are other ways in which some businesses keep their information; the biggest mistake is just to ignore this aspect of business activity.

Calculating cash flow

Try this

A small manufacturing business has just £5,000 in total as cash and a bank deposit. Its forecast of income for the next three months is £ 20,000 then £35,000 then £45,000. Forecast payments to be made are £30,000 each month. Turn this data into a cash flow forecast. Is the business solvent? Does it seem profitable on the basis of the data shown? Should it try to keep a 'reserve' balance? How could this be done?

Poor cash flow management can undermine a basically profitable business. Mark, for example, was unrealistically optimistic about when his customers would pay up and spent on expansion, in the false expectation that money owed to him would arrive before needed. Businesses need to be sure that they **Working** have sufficient working capital to bridge the gap between spending on costs and receiving revenue. Crafty **capital** cash flow management can help unprofitable businesses to survive until their fortunes improve or creditors lose patience. In such situations, tax authorities are sometimes first to take action on late or missing payments and to force insolvency.

One popular saying is that *"turnover is vanity, profit is sanity but cash is reality"*. An alternative version simply suggests that cash is king. Paying attention to cash flow is essential for a business. Most businesses aim not just to cover outgoings but also to maintain a reserve against unexpected problems. One influence on the best size of this reserve is how stable the market is.

Insolvency occurs when a business fails because a lack of working capital means that debts cannot be paid.

Cash flow forecast – a month by month prediction of the timing of expected cash inflows and outflows for a business.

Cash inflows – money received by a business. This includes revenue, investment and borrowing.

Cash outflows – money leaving a business. This includes fixed and variable costs as well as cash withdrawals by the business owner(s).

Liquidity – having sufficient cash available, sometimes also having assets which can quickly be converted to cash.

 WATCH OUT!

A business can be profitable but can fail because of poor cash flow management. Make sure you are clear on the difference between *working capital* and *profit*.

Abuse of power?

Delayed payments

Some countries legally limit the time for which businesses can delay their payments. In France, for example, the limit is two months. Other countries have no such limits, and court action to enforce payment is likely to be expensive and slow. Large firms can take advantage of this by delaying payments to small suppliers who depend on business with them. This improves the cash flow position of the large business at the expense of its smaller suppliers.

> **Example**
> In 2014 Mars ($33bn revenue in 2014) introduced a plan to extend the period UK suppliers wait for payment from 60 to 120 days. It also announced a "supply chain finance scheme" which would allow suppliers to pay 'fees' and obtain speedier payment. According to thisismoney.co.uk, one supplier said "I'm really p***** off. We were told of the plan and figured we would just have to sign up or lose the business. They are releasing a massive chunk of working capital for themselves and their suppliers are paying for it."

Retailers often have the advantage that customers make immediate payment for purchases. However, large retailers can still improve their cash flow at the expense of suppliers. In February 2015, the Groceries Code Adjudicator said it had reasonable suspicion that Tesco had breached the industry's code of practice. Amongst the allegations is the suggestion that Tesco delayed payments to suppliers. Many of these suppliers are small and mainly or completely dependent on contracts with Tesco. Making a fuss about delayed payments risks the goodwill and perhaps losing the business of their dominant customer. The Groceries Code Adjudicator sees a large part of its role as protecting small businesses in dealings with larger firms.

As a generalisation, businesses dealing directly with consumers face fewer delays in payment than small businesses selling to larger businesses. For all businesses, though, paying attention to cash flow plays an important part in success and even survival.

> **Exam style question**
> Evaluate the suggestion that insufficient liquidity is a greater threat to small businesses than failure to make a profit.
> *(20 marks)*